PUFFIN BOOKS

INDIAN FOLK-TALES AND LEGENDS

Pratibha Nath is a freelance journalist and a writer of books for children. She has a wide variety of interests, foremost among them being nature, music and gardening. She lives in New Delhi.

PRATIBHA NATH

INDIAN FOLK-TALES AND LEGENDS

PUFFIN BOOKS
An imprint of Penguin Random House

PUFFIN BOOKS

USA | Canada | UK | Ireland | Australia
New Zealand | India | South Africa | China | Singapore

Puffin Books is part of the Penguin Random House group of companies
whose addresses can be found at global.penguinrandomhouse.com

Published by Penguin Random House India Pvt. Ltd
4th Floor, Capital Tower 1, MG Road,
Gurugram 122 002, Haryana, India

First published in Puffin by Penguin Random House India 1995

Copyright © Pratibha Nath 1995

18 17 16 15 14 13

ISBN 9780140380873

Typeset in Garamond by ADDS INDIA, New Delhi

Printed at Repro India Limited

www.penguin.co.in

This is a legitimate digitally printed version of the book and therefore might not
have certain extra finishing on the cover.

To
Malvika, Siddharth and Ishan
with love

Contents

FOLK-TALES

Fifty-Fifty	9
The Two Daughters	14
The Stone Lion	19
A Seer of Lime	26
Rupali Ba	31
The Magic Wrap	36
One into Two	40
Tables Turned	45
Work for the Demon	49
The Qazi of Jaunpur	56
The Secret Valley	62
Enter Mulla Do-Piaza	66
The Ghost That Got Away	71
A Sweet for Khan	77
Adventure by Midnight	81
The Unwanted Guest	86
Why Pigs Are So Dirty	90
A Trip to Heaven	95

LEGENDS

The Pandavas in the Forest	102
Vishwamitra	110
How Ganga Came Down to Earth	116
Ganapati and Kuber	122
The Thirteenth Year	127
Ram and the Squirrel	137
The God Ayyappan	141

Dronacharya   146
A Gift of Flour   151
Agastya   156
Bhim and Hanuman   161
Bhasmasura   166

Fifty-Fifty

This story comes to us from the Punjab. Like the other states of India, the Punjab also has a good stock of folk-tales. Most of these tales are set in the countryside and deal with the lives of farmers and small-time businessmen. They centre around simple, everyday themes like family ties and friendship, or else greed and dishonesty. In the end justice is done and the wrongdoer suitably punished. But the person wronged does not always need to go to court. Sometimes he obtains justice through his own efforts. Thus these tales illustrate the value of self-reliance. They tell us, too, that we must not be foolish and lose what is ours by right.

*

Two men lived in a village. One was called Banta Singh, the other Ghanta Singh. The two were the best of friends. They enjoyed each other's company and spent all their time together. But there was one big difference between them. While Ghanta Singh was a cunning fellow, always on the lookout for some benefit to himself, Banta Singh was a simpleton. He blindly said yes to any scheme that came from Ghanta Singh. He never stopped to consider whether the scheme was fair to him.

Neither Banta Singh nor Ghanta Singh had much money. Naturally, they did not have many possessions either. In fact they did without a lot of things. One day Ghanta Singh came up with a bright new idea. 'Bhai Banta Singh, I have a suggestion. A brilliant suggestion. Will you agree to it?'

'But of course,' said Banta Singh. 'Have I ever said no to any of your suggestions?'

'Very good,' said Ghanta Singh. 'I suggest we share all our possessions on a fifty-fifty basis.'

Delighted with the idea, Banta Singh grabbed Ghanta Singh's hand and shook it so hard that his friend's bones began to rattle. 'Splendid!' cried Banta Singh. 'Where shall we begin?'

Ghanta Singh thought for a moment. 'Look here, we have three things that are very precious to us. I have a cow, you have a nice warm blanket and a ber (wood apple) tree behind your house. I suggest we share these three things fifty-fifty.'

'Sure, sure,' agreed Banta Singh. 'How shall we go about it?'

Ghanta Singh had it all worked out. He said, 'Since you are such a good friend, I'll give you the first share in everything. You take the front half of the cow, I'll take the rear. You take the roots and trunk of the tree, I'll be content with the leaves and branches. And as for the blanket, you keep it all day, my friend. Honest I don't need it. . . .'

Banta Singh was quick to protest. 'Why shouldn't you use the blanket too?' he asked. 'That's not fair.'

'Oh, all right,' said Ghanta Singh. 'If you insist, I'll take the blanket at night.' And so things were finally settled, to the great satisfaction of both.

A week went by, then two. Soon it was a month since the new arrangement had been put into practice. And slowly it began to dawn on Banta Singh that something was wrong. Since he owned the front half of the cow, it was his job to wake up at the crack of dawn and feed the animal. He had to draw a bucket of water from the well so the cow had fresh, clean water to drink twice a day. But the rear of the cow belonged to Ghanta Singh so it was he who milked it. He drank a whole tumblerful of rich, creamy milk every morning. But all Banta Singh had was tea in a glass only slightly larger than a thimble.

As for the blanket, it lay on Banta Singh's bed all day. But he could not use it because he was up and about, attending to his

business. When night fell, Ghanta Singh whipped away the blanket and snuggled under it. Meanwhile Banta Singh had to spend the night curled up into a ball to keep himself warm.

Banta Singh had hoped to eat the ber from his tree. For months he had looked after the tree, removing weeds, hoeing the soil and adding manure when it was needed. The fruit formed on the branches and grew before his eyes. But when the first ber was ripe — whoosh! Ghanta Singh reached out and grabbed it. And pop it went into his mouth!

'What about me?' asked Banta Singh.

'Listen, my friend,' said Ghanta Singh patiently, 'wasn't it settled that the branches belonged to me? And where did I find this ber? On a branch, of course. So it's mine and that's that.'

Banta Singh was most annoyed but he couldn't do a thing about it, so he went for a long walk. On and on he walked till he came to the forest near his village. There he met a sadhu with matted hair and holy ash rubbed all over his body. The sadhu looked at Banta Singh. 'What's the matter, my son?' he asked. 'You look unhappy. Tell me everything. I might be able to help you.'

Banta Singh told him the whole story. The sadhu said, 'My son, you've been fooled all this time. Why did you allow your friend to cheat you like this?'

'What shall I do now?' asked Banta Singh.

'I'll tell you,' said the sadhu. And he told Banta Singh in detail how to get even with his friend.

Banta Singh came home feeling very bright and cheerful. As soon as the two friends had finished their evening meal, Ghanta Singh said, 'I'm sleepy. Get me the blanket, will you?'

'Sure,' said Banta Singh. He picked up the blanket, soaked it in water and handed it over to Ghanta Singh. 'What?' screamed Ghanta Singh. 'What do you mean by this? Why did you soak the blanket in water?'

'You forget, Bhai Ghanta Singh, the blanket is mine by day and I can do with it exactly as I feel.'

Ghanta Singh was so surprised that his mouth dropped open. What had happened to Banta Singh? But he said nothing. He only grumbled himself to sleep, though he was cold and miserable all night.

Next morning Ghanta Singh got up early and hurried out to milk the cow. Banta Singh was already awake. He had fed the cow and given her fresh water to drink. But he was still hanging around. Ghanta Singh placed a pail between his knees and began to milk the cow. When the pail was half full, Banta Singh tickled the cow's nose with a wisp of straw. Startled, the cow kicked hard. Not only did she upset the pail, she landed Ghanta Singh a good crack on the jaw.

Ghanta Singh lost his temper. 'Why did you tickle the cow just when I was milking her?' he shouted. 'Didn't you know she would kick out?'

'Of course I did,' came the reply. 'But the front half of the cow is mine and I can do with it exactly as I please'. To this Ghanta Singh could make no reply. That morning he missed his tumbler of milk. All he had was tea in a glass only slightly larger than a thimble.

When the sun rose a little higher, Ghanta Singh went and sat in the fork of the ber tree. He began to pick and eat the fruits one by one. Suddenly Banta Singh appeared with an axe. Ghanta Singh cried out in alarm, 'For heaven's sake, don't chop down the tree or we'll have no more fruit to eat.'

Banta Singh laughed. 'You forget,' he said, 'the trunk is mine. If I wish to chop it down, you can't stop me.'

At last Ghanta Singh realized that he could not cheat his friend any longer. 'Let's change the arrangement,' he said. 'This time you decide how we should share things.'

Banta Singh had it all worked out. 'We'll use the blanket on alternate nights. Is that all right? We'll both look after the cow and share the milk equally. As for the tree, we'll take turns looking after that as well. And when the fruit comes, we'll share it fifty-fifty.'

Ghanta Singh readily agreed to this new arrangement. He was happy to share things with Banta Singh and the two became good friends once again.

The Two Daughters

The following is a story about the Kurava tribe which lives in Kerala. For the most part the Kuravas are a simple people, untouched by modern civilization. They earn a meagre living through agriculture and cattle rearing. This story presents a very realistic picture of an old time Kurava.

*

Once there was an old man who lived in a village in Kerala. His home was a thatched hut surrounded by coconut trees. He belonged to the Kurava tribe and like other members of his tribe, he was a poor and simple man.

The old Kurava had two daughters who had both been married off into families of modest means. The elder son-in-law continued to be poor. But the younger one started a business that flourished and he soon became a rich man.

The old Kurava and his wife were totally unaware of this. They lived in their small hut, cut off from the outside world. They tilled their fields and ate two simple meals of coarse rice every day. Their bed was no more than a length of sacking spread out on the floor of the hut. But the Kurava and his wife were content. The riches of the world meant nothing to them.

One day Kurava's wife told him, 'We have married off our daughters but we have no idea how they are. They haven't come home for a whole year and we haven't gone to see them either. Why don't you go and meet them and find out if they are happy or if something is bothering them?'

The old Kurava readily agreed to go. He set out at daybreak the following morning, carrying nothing but his umbrella and a bunch

of home-grown plantains. The older daughter's village was nearer, being half a day's walk away, so he decided to go there first.

The Kurava arrived at his daughter's house at midday. He found her living in a hut much like his own. It had a thatched roof which extended beyond the front door to form a veranda. And in this veranda the daughter did all her cooking. When the Kurava arrived, a pot of rice was boiling on the fire. The older daughter sat chopping a pumpkin from the vine that grew at the back of the hut. She welcomed her father warmly. They both sat in the veranda and shared a meal of rice with salt, pumpkin curry and fiery red chillies. The old Kurava washed at the village pond and slept soundly on a length of sacking spread out on the floor. His older daughter's home reminded him so much of his own that he loved it and felt perfectly at peace.

The following morning the old Kurava went back home. His wife was waiting anxiously for him. 'Don't you worry,' the Kurava told her. 'Our older daughter is very happy. Indeed she is very lucky to have such a good home.' And the two spent the rest of the day talking about the good fortune of their elder daughter.

A few days went by and then the Kurava's wife said again, 'You have been to see our older daughter. Why don't you go and see the younger one too and find out if she is happy or if something is bothering her?'

Once again the old Kurava readily agreed to go. He set out at daybreak with his umbrella and a couple of home-grown coconuts in his bag. It was evening before he arrived at the prosperous village where his daughter lived. He asked for his son-in-law by name and people directed him to a grand looking, double-storeyed house with an iron gate. The Kurava shook his head at the very sight. 'No, no, this can't be my daughter's house,' said he. But it was. His daughter came running to greet him and led him in. She made him sit in a chair with a cushion under him and another one behind his back. The Kurava was most uncomfortable. He had never used cushions in his life so he removed both. But his troubles had only just begun.

Soon it was time for the evening meal. The Kurava would have been perfectly happy to sit cross-legged on the floor and eat off a plantain leaf. But there was another chair waiting for him. Worse, the food was set out on a table. There were no plantain leaves either, but gleaming metal thalis (plates) heaped with fine white rice and several bowls of steaming hot food. The Kurava was dazed. He asked for a green chilli, helped himself to a single piece of fish, sprinkled a little salt on his rice and began to race through his meal. But his daughter and son-in-law kept coaxing him to eat more and more. And he ended up eating at one meal more than he ever ate in two days. The food was rich and spicy too and did not feel good inside him.

The Kurava staggered out of his chair. His daughter now led him to his bedroom. Right in the middle of the room there was a bed. And over this bed hung a mosquito net, tied to four wooden poles. The Kurava thought he had to sleep on top of the mosquito net. Climbing the poles was no problems for a man who had spent a lifetime climbing coconut trees. But when he lay down on top, the mosquito net collapsed. And with a loud thud the Kurava fell on the mattress below. He was not hurt, but the noise brought the entire household running to his room. They somehow managed to hide their smiles. But try as they might, the Kurava would not sleep on the bed again. It was the floor for him or nothing.

Day dawned. Before the poor harassed Kurava had recovered from the adventures of the previous night, his daughter came to his room. She brought him some tooth powder to clean his teeth. The Kurava had always used a fresh green twig for the purpose. He thought the powder was meant to be eaten so he popped all of it into his mouth. And how he coughed and coughed till his daughter came running again with a glass of water!

But by then the Kurava had had enough. He felt that it was dangerous for him to stay in that house any longer. So he grabbed his umbrella, bade everyone a hasty goodbye and set out for home.

At the sight of him, his wife jumped up. 'How is our daughter?' cried she, full of excitement. 'Tell me, how is she?'

The Kurava wiped the perspiration from his forehead, sighed and sat down. 'Our younger daughter is in great trouble,' said he. 'She doesn't even have a straw mat to sit on. In the morning she has to eat a fistful of some horrible tasting powder. Ugh! It's enough to kill your appetite for a day. And the food! The curries are floating in oil and one is forced to eat to bursting.'

His wife stared at him in shock and disbelief. 'Really?' she whispered. 'Oh my poor daughter!'

'Wait,' said the Kurava. 'That is not all. The nights are the worst. One must climb and sleep on a strange looking bed. Believe me, only a monkey could do it. Thank heavens I managed to escape without breaking my limbs.'

The old Kurava and his wife spread a length of sacking on the floor and went to sleep. But their thoughts were with their younger daughter who did not have the good fortune to be able to sleep on the floor.

The Stone Lion

The district of Lahaul-Spiti forms part of the state of Himachal. It is a high altitude desert where vegetation is limited. In particular, there are very few trees. Most people living in Lahaul-Spiti are shepherds belonging to the Gaddi tribe. During summer they graze their flocks on the mountain slopes of the district. But before the onset of winter, they move down to the lower hills of Kullu. This is because the winter in Lahaul-Spiti is bitterly cold and life almost comes to a standstill. People who do stay on during winter are confined to their homes. And that is when they spin wool and weave or knit shawls and other garments. They also while away their time telling stories. Here is one such story.

*

People say it happened more than a hundred years ago, Among the high mountains of Lahaul-Spiti there was a small village. You could call it a village. But in truth it was no more than a cluster of five or six huts tucked away in the fold of a hill. One of these huts stood apart from the others and in this hut lived a boy named Ranchen.

Ranchen lived alone. He had no family — father, mother, brother or sister. So he led a lonely life. But Ranchen was by nature a very cheerful boy. Slim, brown and merry-eyed, he was also blessed with a rich voice. As he walked up and down the mountain paths, Ranchen sang aloud, for it brought him great happiness. People loved to hear him sing because it made them happy too. But there was one person who did not like to hear him sing, and that was Wangu, the oldest man in the village. Wangu was quite the opposite of Ranchen. He was quarrelsome, grumpy and greedy. He did not like to see anyone happy. All he wanted was more money, more land and more sheep to his flock. Nobody liked Wangu.

The people in Ranchen's village were Gaddis. They were shepherds and earned their living by rearing sheep. Ranchen also owned a flock of sheep, some thirty in number. Ranchen sold the wool from his sheep. Sometimes, when he needed more money, he also sold a sheep. He had enough of sattu (roasted and pounded grain) to eat, two warm woollen tunics to wear and a roof over his head. More than that Ranchen did not desire. Early in the morning he took his sheep out to graze. Well before dark he was back. Locking up his sheep for the night, he ate his sattu, sat around humming for a while and finally fell asleep. It was a simple, hard life without any comforts, but Ranchen was perfectly happy with his lot.

Ranchen always took his sheep out to graze in a pasture near his village. One day he thought, 'The grass in this pasture has become very sparse. It looks as if my sheep don't get their fill. I must find another pasture.'

The following day Ranchen woke up very early. He took his staff and enough sattu for his midday meal. Then he called out to his sheep. Singing at the top of his voice as he led his sheep, Ranchen set out.

After walking for about an hour, Ranchen climbed a hill. And right there before him lay a deep valley. Here and there in the valley were remnants of a broken stone wall. They seemed to be part of an old palace that had once stood there. The walls were surrounded by grass, so lush and green that Ranchen was thrilled at the sight. 'This is the place for me,' thought he with great joy. 'Here my sheep can eat their fill right through summer.'

Ranchen left his sheep to graze and began to roam around. When it was time to have his midday meal, he climbed up one side of the valley from where he could keep an eye on his sheep. He was looking for a suitable place to sit when something caught his eye. A few paces away, on an outcrop of yellowish rock, stood a lion. It had been carved out of the rock but it had been done so well that it looked real. Its mouth was closed but the eyes were wide open. It seemed that the lion was the sentinel of the valley and had kept watch over it for hundreds of years.

Ranchen was a friendly boy. He loved to talk to people. He went and sat near the lion. 'Brother lion,' he said, 'I have come to chat with you. You are all alone in this world and so am I. Why don't we become friends?'

Naturally, the stone lion said nothing, but Ranchen went on, 'You don't know me at all so first I must tell you all about myself.' And he told the stone lion everything about himself, where he lived, how he had lost his parents, and how he reared sheep to earn his living. When the story was over, Ranchen put an arm around the lion and said, 'Come now, let's eat. I didn't know you were here or I would have bought more sattu. But never mind, we'll share what there is.'

Ranchen opened his bundle of sattu and placed a little before the lion. Then he ate his own share and went down the hill to mind his sheep. Well before sundown he took leave of the lion, herded his sheep together and left for his village.

Ranchen was very pleased with himself. He had not only found a pasture for his sheep, he had also found a new friend. Now he went to the valley every day. While his sheep grazed their fill, Ranchen sat near the stone lion and chatted to his heart's content. When it was time to eat, Ranchen shared his sattu with the lion. He knew it was the birds who ate the sattu and not the lion. But it gave him great satisfaction to know that he had shared with his friend. At the end of the day, Ranchen took leave of the lion and went back home, singing all the way.

Three or four months went by in this manner and then the weather began to change. The sun no longer felt so warm and the nights were much colder. Winter was coming. And winter in Lahaul-Spiti was very harsh. So everyone in Ranchen's village was getting ready to go down to the lower hills of Kullu valley. All the villagers went together, their sheep in one large flock, for there was safety in numbers. Together they could fight the dangers on the way—robbers , snowstorms and wild animals. They spent the long nights together, huddled around a fire, somewhere on a mountainside. One man kept watch while the others snatched some sleep. Ranchen did not wish to be parted from his newfound friend, the stone lion But he knew the importance of going down to the Kullu valley with the others. Finally he made up his mind to go.

The following morning Ranchen went to see the stone lion. 'Brother lion,' he said, 'in a few days' time I must leave you and go down to Kullu valley. I don't want to go, but I simply must or else my flocks and I will freeze to death. Tell me, dear lion, you *will* miss me a little, won't you?' To Ranchen's utter amazement, the lion opened its mouth and replied, 'Brother Ranchen, I'm going to miss you very much. But the winter months will soon be over and then you'll be back and we can be together again. But before you go, let me tell you something. I'm delighted to have you as my friend. I wish to make you a little gift. . .'

Ranchen spoke quickly, 'No no, I have everything I could possibly need. A flock of sheep, a home to live in and my fill of sattu everyday. What more could I wish for?'

'Listen to me,' said the lion. 'I want you to come here tomorrow morning, as soon as the eastern sky begins to turn light. Bring a bag with you. You'll find my mouth wide open. Thrust your hand in and fill your bag with whatever you find inside my mouth. But remember, this must be done before sunrise. As soon as the sun peeps over those hills, my mouth will close.'

Ranchen laughed. 'Brother lion, what are you going to give me? Do tell me.' But the lion's mouth had snapped shut and Ranchen had no choice but to collect his sheep and go back home.

Early next morning Ranchen was fast asleep when a rook flew over his hut and called. Ranchen shot up in bed, suddenly wide awake. He threw off his quilt and ran to the window. The eastern sky had just began to turn light. His friend would be waiting.

Ranchen ran all the way and arrived at the valley completely out of breath. The stone lion was waiting. 'Where's the bag?' he asked. 'I'm in a hurry. I asked you to bring a bag.'

Ranchen drew his breath in sharply. 'I forgot all about the bag,' said he. 'But never mind. My cap will do.'

He took off his cap and without a moment's hesitation, thrust his hand into the lion's mouth. When he withdrew his hand, it was full of gold nuggets. Just then the sun cleared the edge of the tallest hill and the lion's mouth shut tight. Ranchen thanked the lion. Covering the cap with one hand, he went back home as happy as he could be.

Ranchen had almost reached his village when he ran into old Wangu who was taking his sheep out to graze. Wangu squarely blocked Ranchen's path. 'Where have you been?' he demanded. 'And what are you hiding there?' He pushed Ranchen's hand away roughly. The gold nuggets dazzled Wangu's eyes, but only for a moment. He leapt at Ranchen and grabbed him by the neck. 'So you've been robbing people, eh? Tell me the truth at once or I'll report you to the headman of the village. . . .'

At the very mention of the headman, Ranchen got scared. And out came the whole story. He even showed Wangu the way to the valley of the stone lion. Wangu was delighted. As soon as Ranchen began to pack his belongings to go down to Kullu, Wangu began his visits to the valley.

He went every day. And he always carried delicacies for the stone lion. A bowl of yak butter, as white as freshly fallen snow. Or a jar of clear, golden honey gathered from the hives of rock bees. He took freshly roasted, hand-pounded sattu and a leather bottle full of rich, creamy milk. He took all these things, placed them before the lion, bowed with folded hands and stood on one side. 'O king of the land of Lahaul-Spiti,' he said addressing the lion, 'please forgive me for not coming to pay obeisance to you earlier. Foolish and ignorant that I am, I did not even know that you were here, or would I have stayed away so long? Great one, please take pity on your devoted servant. Be so kind as to accept the humble offering that I have placed at your feet.'

Sometimes Wangu took a fan made of yak's tail and stood beside the lion, fanning away flies and insects. And he talked incessantly, trying to please the lion with flattery. But the lion simply would not open its mouth.

This went on for a week or more. The weather was becoming colder by the day and the villagers had left with their flocks. But Wangu stuck on. His family begged of him to accompany them to Kullu but he refused, and in the end they left without him. Now Wangu was alone. As grey clouds gathered in the sky, he began to get desperate. Did the stone lion really give nuggets of gold? Or had Ranchen cooked up the whole story to get out of Wangu's clutches?

But finally Wangu's patience was rewarded. One day he placed a bowl of porridge before the lion and said, 'O king of this noble land, please partake of my humble offering. It is not worthy of you . . .'

'Oh, but it is,' said a voice. 'And I thank you for looking after me all these days.' To his utter amazement, Wangu realized that it was the stone lion who spoke. He was overjoyed. The lion went on, 'I want you to come here tomorrow morning, as soon as the eastern sky begins to turn light. Bring a bag with you. You will find my mouth wide open. Thrust your hand in and fill your bag with whatever you find inside my mouth. But remember, this must be done before sunrise. As soon as the sun peeps over those hills, my mouth will close.'

Wangu went home dancing for joy. He rummaged around and found a stout bag, used for storing grain. He cleaned and dusted the bag. That night he went to bed with the bag beside him but he was too excited to sleep. When the night was far gone Wangu thought, 'The stone lion told me to complete the job before sunrise. But one thing is quite clear: the earlier I go, the more time I shall have to pick up gold nuggets. So why don't I go right away?'

It must have been around four in the morning when Wangu set out for the valley. He wore a thick woollen cloak and a cap that covered everything save his eyes. In one hand he carried a staff, in the other a lantern. The bag hung from one shoulder. An icy wind was blowing down the mountain and the sky was overcast. But Wangu was sure of the way. After all, he had been born among these very hills and had spent his entire life there . . . .

For some time he continued in the right direction. And then suddenly he stubbed his foot against a rock. Wangu stumbled and rolled down the hill. He was not hurt but his lantern was smashed to pieces. It was pitch dark. Wangu walked and walked but without the lantern he could not find his way again. When day dawned he had wandered far, far away from the valley of the stone lion and was hopelessly lost. To this day, nobody knows what happened to Wangu.

A Seer of Lime

Akbar, the great Mughal emperor, was known to value men of learning and wit. Just as Indian jewellers make ornaments studded with nine different precious stones called 'navratna' (nine gems), Akbar had at his court a group of nine brilliant men known as his Navratnas. Birbal was one of the nine. He was a very shrewd, practical, down-to-earth person. But his greatest asset was his ability to utter a bitter truth in the politest manner, adding a touch of humour to make it acceptable. Birbal will always be remembered for his common sense and wit. With the help of these qualities, he often made the emperor see the folly of his actions. Time and again he rebuked Akbar but never annoyed him enough to earn the death penalty. Till the end he lived at the court as Raja Birbal, a rich and highly respected man, one of Akbar's favourites.

*

When Akbar ruled over the Mughal empire in India, his capital was the old, historic city of Agra. The royal family and many of the courtiers lived in the Agra fort. At the back of the fort was a maze of narrow, winding lanes where the common people lived. In one of these lanes stood a paan (betel leaf) shop owned by a man named Ismail. The shop was small but the paans served were unforgettable. Ismail served sherbet (cold drinks) too—keora, gulab and sandal. There was a string cot permanently placed in front of the shop so people could relax while they sipped the sherbet and enjoyed the paan.

One day a stranger came to Ismail's shop. It was a very hot afternoon and the stranger looked tired. Ismail gave him a tumbler of cold water to drink and asked him, 'Do you live in this city?'

The stranger shook his head. 'I don't,' said he. 'I have come from a long way off and am staying at a serai (inn) two lanes away.'

'What brings you here?' asked Ismail. The stranger sat down on the string cot in front of the shop. 'Ah,' said he, 'I have come to see if the great emperor Akbar will accept me as one of his courtiers.'

'Accept you as one of his courtiers?' said Ismail with some surprise. 'That is a great honour. Very few people get such an honour.'

'I know,' said the stranger. 'But still I wish to try my luck.'

Day in and day out the stranger came to Ismail's shop, sat on the cot and chatted for a while. He was a widely travelled man, very intelligent and witty. But he seemed restless, with little to do and always waiting for the day when he would get a position at court.

One day the stranger came as usual, asked for a glass of sherbet and sat down on the cot. He had barely taken a couple of sips when a man came running down the lane and stopped abruptly in front of Ismail's shop. He was panting hard and seemed to be in a tearing hurry. 'Quick, Ismail Bhai,' said the man, 'give me a seer of lime as quick as you can.'

Ismail laughed. 'What's the hurry?' he ashed. 'It is too hot to be hurrying around. And you're quite out of breath, anyway. Why don't you sit down and rest for a while?'

'No, no,' said the man. 'This is no time to rest. Give me a seer of lime, for heaven's sake. And look sharp about it too!'

All this time the stranger had been looking on, curiosity writ large on his face. Now he stood up and said, in a voice of authority,

'Wait a minute, wait a minute. What do you want a seer of lime for? Nobody buys so much lime at one go.'

'You're right,' replied the man. 'The truth is, *I* don't want the lime. The great Emperor Akbar has asked me to get it.'

'Really? The emperor has asked you to get it?' repeated the stranger. 'Do you work for the emperor then?'

The man drew himself up to his full height and answered proudly, 'Indeed I do. I make a paan for His Majesty after each meal, wrap it in gold leaf and serve it to him on a gold platter. Today, after the midday meal was over, His Majesty took a paan as usual. Next minute he turned around and told me, "Go to the bazar right away and bring a seer of lime."'

The stranger went on, 'Did His Majesty seem annoyed when he said this?'

'How can I tell? When the great emperor talks to you, you're not supposed to look up and see his face.'

'I see,' said the stranger, nodding his head. 'Take my advice. Don't buy lime. Buy a seer of curd instead.'

'How can I?' replied the man. 'You don't expect me to disobey the emperor?'

'Of course not. As a rule you must never disobey the emperor. But if you obey him this time, your life is in danger.' At this the man was scared out of his wits. He bought a seer of curd from a halwai's shop and hurried back to the fort.

Akbar took one look at the man and demanded, 'Have you got the lime? Good. Now sit there and eat it.' While Akbar went back to court, the man lifted the earthen pot of curd and happily drank it up. 'Praise be to Allah I bought curd and not lime,' thought he. 'A seer of lime would surely have been the end of me!'

The following morning the man was back at work. At the sight of him Akbar turned purple with rage. 'Did you or did you not eat that seer of lime?' he roared. 'No man can survive a seer of lime in his stomach. How come you are still alive?'

The poor man fell at Akbar's feet and told him the whole story. Akbar was not one to lose time. He immediately sent his men to Ismail's shop and, in less than an hour, the mysterious stranger was standing in the royal durbar, facing Akbar, the great Mughal emperor. Akbar was seated on his throne. He looked majestic in his silken robes and jewel-studded crown. He had a commanding voice as well. But the stranger seemed perfectly relaxed. 'Do you know why you've been called here?' Akbar asked.

'I do, Jahanpanah (a royal title meaning 'Refuge of the World').'

'Why did you tell our servant to buy curd instead of lime?'

The stranger bowed his head. 'Jahanpanah, I was surprised to see a man buying a whole seer of lime. He told me it was his job to prepare paan for Your Majesty I knew at once that he must have put too much lime in the paan and the royal tongue must have been cut. As a punishment Your Majesty wished him to eat a whole seer of lime.'

'Very well,' said Akbar, impressed by the stranger's powers of reasoning. 'What you thought was correct. But what right had you to prevent our servant from obeying the royal order?'

The stranger bowed his head again. 'Forgive me, Jahanpanah, I had no right at all. I simply wished to save the life of an innocent man. And I also wished to prevent Your Majesty from taking the life of an innocent man in a fit of anger.'

'What is your name?' asked Akbar.

'Birbal, Your Majesty.'

Akbar smiled. 'We are pleased with you. We need wise and fearless men like you to help us rule over our vast empire. From today you shall occupy a place of honour in our court!' Delighted beyond words, Birbal bent right down to the floor and salaamed the emperor. And that is how the famous wit Birbal first entered the court of Akbar.

Rupali Ba

From the state of Gujarat comes this story of a brave woman. Long ago many Rajputs from Rajputana (present day Rajasthan) settled down in Gujarat and became one with the local people, the Gujjars. Rajput men and women are famous for their bravery and sense of honour. Their presence in Gujarat is one reason why Gujarati folklore is so full of tales of heroism.

*

In olden days in Gujarat, people travelled from one place to another on foot. Sometimes they rode on camels or in carts drawn by bullocks or horses. Journeys took a long time, as men and animals moved slowly through desert and plain. There were only a few small villages dotting the countryside. People travelled by day, and when night fell they took shelter in some wayside inn. But if there was no inn on the way, they travelled right through the night, guided by the stars.

Journeys were not only tiring, they were extremely dangerous as well. Bands of robbers and outlaws roamed the countryside on fast horses. They waylaid travellers and took away their jewellery and other valuables. If a traveller offered resistance, a dagger plunged into him did the trick. No wonder common people were unwilling to travel. And when they did venture out of their homes, they took an escort. These escorts were brave and tough men whose profession it was to safeguard the lives and property of people travelling from one village to another. Every village had its own escorts and they were in great demand.

Gema was one such escort. He had made a name for himself as a man of courage and daring. In particular he wielded a sword with exceptional skill. Gema was so greatly feared that robbers ran away at the very mention of his name. They never came near a travelling group if Gema happened to be escorting them.

Gema was aware of the fact that he was famous. In time he also grew proud of it. The praise that he received as an escort went straight to his head. He would boast about it. 'Don't you know who I am?' he asked. 'I'm Gema, bravest of the brave, the all-powerful.' Or he would say, 'Gema is known all over. When a robber's wife wishes to frighten her children to sleep she tells them "Gema is coming". And they immediately close their eyes.' And so it happened that Gema slowly became a little less alert when escorting travellers.

In Gema's village there lived a young and pretty Rajput woman named Rupali Ba. She was newly married and lived with her in-laws. Once Gema was engaged to escort Rupali Ba to her father's place in another village. They had to travel through country that was completely deserted, with nothing but sand and a few bushes as far as the eye could see. It was a risky trip all right. To top it all, the custom of the times demanded that a new bride should be wearing a whole lot of gold and silver jewellery. And Rupali Ba was a new bride. Since she had married into a well-to-do family, she would also be carrying a bag of gold coins and some expensive clothes.

On the appointed day, two carts drawn by bullocks set out from the village. In the first sat Rupali Ba, with all her belongings. In the second came Gema, carrying his weapons and food and water for the journey.

They travelled all day, with but a short break when they sat in the shade of a rock and had their midday meal. Evening found them still travelling and still nowhere near an inn. As night came on, Gema fell asleep, forgetting all about his duties as an escort. The driver of the cart shook him several times and said, 'Wake up

Gema, wake up please. Darkness has fallen and it isn't safe to sleep now.'

But Gema was too proud of himself to take note of the warning. 'Stop bothering me,' he mumbled in his sleep. 'What are you afraid of? You have the great Gema with you. Just drive on.'

Their words carried far on the silent desert air. Seated in the front cart, surrounded by a fine muslin curtain, Rupali Ba heard them. 'Gema,' she called out, 'don't sleep now. This is the time to keep watch. It's dark and lonely and there's not a soul around.' But Gema did not care. He slept comfortably as the vehicles creaked on.

Suddenly the driver of the second cart gave Gema a push. 'Wake up, for heaven's sake. I can see lights in the distance. Aren't you supposed to protect the woman from danger?' But the only reply he received was a sleepy, 'Gema is never afraid. Let them come, I say. Remember I am Gema.'

The lights kept coming nearer and nearer. The drivers were in a panic but what could they do? Suddenly a dozen men burst upon them. Armed to the teeth, and carrying flaming torches, they looked terrifying indeed. They surrounded the cart and pounced on the sleeping Gema. Before Gema was fully awake, his arms and legs were firmly tied with string. The robbers then passed a stick under his knees and tied him to it so he became like a ball. Gema was now completely helpless. The robbers gave him a hard push and he went rolling in the sand till he got stuck in a clump of thorny bushes.

Having got rid of Gema, the robbers turned their attention to Rupali Ba. The leader of the gang approached the first cart. 'Hand over all your valuables,' he demanded. Rupali Ba gave him the bag of gold coins. But the robber was not satisfied. 'Hand over all the ornaments you're wearing,' he told her. 'Down to your anklets.' Those days it was a matter of honour even among thieves and robbers not to take away the ornaments that a woman was wearing. But these robbers had no sense of honour.

Rupali Ba did not lose her nerve. She quietly removed her ornaments and gave them to the robber. Then she informed him calmly, 'My anklets are made of solid silver. They are strong and heavy and I can't possibly remove them. But you may take them off yourself, if you so wish.' And Rupali Ba pushed out her two feet from under the muslin curtain. Two of the robbers immediately got down to work removing the anklets. While their attention was thus diverted, Rupali Ba groped around her for a weapon. At the back of the cart she found a pole. Gripping it with both hands, she brought the pole crashing down on the two heads bent over her feet. And that was the end of the two robbers.

Rupali Ba leapt out of her cart. She forgot that she was a woman and that the men before her were extremely tough and cruel. She now had a weapon and was determined to teach the robbers a lesson. Rupali Ba went for them, hitting right and left with the long pole, wielding it as though it were a slender bamboo stick. So fierce was her attack that nobody looking at her would have believed that she was only eighteen. Rupali Ba fought like a true Rajput woman, brave and utterly fearless.

The robbers were taken completely by surprise. Having got rid of Gema, they did not expect anyone to resist them so they had put away their swords. Rupali Ba made the most of this opportunity while she could. But soon the robbers snatched up their swords again and returned the attack. Time and again they hit Rupali Ba and blood flowed freely from her wounds. But she did not give up till at last the robber chief decided he had had enough. He turned and fled from the scene, followed by the five or six survivors of his gang.

In the meantime Gema had managed to untie his ropes. But he was so ashamed of himself that he disappeared into the desert and never showed his face again.

Rupali Ba did not climb back into her cart. She told the drivers to go on while she followed them on foot. In her right hand she carried a sword that one of the robbers had dropped as he fled. For the rest of the night, no robber dared come near her for fear of being cut to pieces.

In time they arrived at a village belonging to Rupali Ba's uncle who loved her like his own daughter. He offered her some kasumbo (a drink made from opium) to ease her pain. She took it and walked on to her father's village. But by the time Rupali Ba reached home, her strength was completely drained. She had lost a lot of blood and just about managed to say a few words to her parents. A few hours later she was dead.

To this day the villagers of Gujarat remember Rupali Ba. They love to retell the story of her fight with the robbers and to sing songs in praise of that brave young Rajput girl.

The Magic Wrap

The state of Assam is home to many tribes. Each tribe has its own traditional customs and beliefs and its own treasury of folk-tales. The following is a folk-tale popular among the Garo tribe of Assam. The Garos call themselves Achik-mande, meaning 'Men of the Hills'. They believe that their original homeland was Tibet. Nobody knows when this story was first told, but it has been doing the rounds for generations.

*

In a village of Assam there once lived a chief of the Garo tribe. His ancestors had been chiefs before him, so he was a rich man. His house was made of the sturdiest bamboo in the land while its doors and windows were draped with the finest cane matting. Silk carpets lay on the floor and copper lamps gleamed from recesses in the walls.

The chief and his wife led a very comfortable life indeed. They loved their home and the beautiful wooded country in which they lived. But most of all they loved their daughter. She was an only child, good natured and lovely to look at. The chief and his wife doted on her.

When the girl grew up, she fell in love with a young man from her own tribe. Her parents liked the boy and the marriage was settled. After marriage, the bride and the groom were to move in with the chief and his wife.

On the eve of the wedding the girl's mother took her aside and said, 'My child, as wedding gifts I'm giving you garments made of the softest silk. I'm also giving you ornaments, made of gold and studded with rubies and emeralds. But one more gift I'm giving you and that, to me, is the most precious of them all.'

36

The mother said something under her breath. Then, unlocking a stout wooden casket, she took out a wrap made of silk and embroidered with a thousand flowers in all the colours of the rainbow. They shone so, they dazzled the eye. 'Oh mother,' cried the girl, stretching out her hand eagerly to touch the wrap. But her mother snatched it away. 'Don't!' she cautioned. 'Don't you touch that wrap before you know the story behind it! This wrap was a gift from a goddess to my great-grandmother, on her wedding day. It has since been handed down from mother to daughter. But it is no ordinary wrap. Before you touch it, you must chant a magic spell that I shall teach you. Remember! A great disaster shall befall anyone who touches that wrap without first chanting the spell!'

The girl soon learnt the spell. She assured her mother that on no account would she touch the wrap without first chanting the spell. When she had admired the wrap to her heart's content, it was replaced inside the casket and securely locked. The following day the girl was married and began to live happily with her husband. But he knew nothing about the secret of the wrap.

The years rolled by. The chief and his wife grew old and died. Their daughter and her husband were left by themselves in the spacious bamboo house. The wrap still remained in the girl's possession. She never wore it for fear of spoiling it. But sometimes she took it out of the casket and held it up so the embroidered flowers caught the light and shone like jewels. Once a year she aired it and locked it right back. She never forgot to chant the spell before touching the wrap. But her husband still did not know what lay inside the casket and never asked.

One day the chief's daughter felt that it was time she aired the wrap. She chanted the magic spell under her breath and unlocked the wooden casket. Then, carefully lifting up the wrap, she spread it out so the gentle mountain air could blow over it. For a while she stood there, unable to tear herself away from the glowing colours. And then suddenly she remembered that her husband had asked for a dish of crabs for his midday meal. Leaving the wrap where it was, she picked up a basket and set out for a nearby stream to look for crabs.

As she hurried down the path to the stream she met her husband. He was coming from a visit to the next village. The chief's daughter told him to keep an eye on the wrap. 'But,' she cautioned, 'on no account are you to touch the wrap! Not even if rain falls in torrents or hailstones come down as big as grapes!'

The husband heard her through, though he did think all that fuss over a mere wrap was quite unnecessary. Soon after his wife had left, black thunderclouds gathered in the sky and it began to rain. The man got worried. He called out to his wife as loud as he could, but the thunder was louder. It completely drowned out his voice. His wife was hurrying home just then but the path was uphill and she could not walk fast enough.

Soon the rain turned to hail. Now the man got really alarmed. Unless he did something about it quick, the wrap would be ruined. Forgetting all about the warning, he rushed out and grabbed the wrap to whisk it away indoors. But oh horrors! The moment he touched the wrap he felt himself change. In a flash he had turned into a large and beautiful male bird, while the brightly coloured wrap turned into his feathers and tail. Just then his wife came rushing in. With a cry she caught hold of the one end of the wrap that remained and tried to snatch it away from her husband. But the moment she touched it, she turned into a female bird.

These two became the peacock and peahen. The man had caught a much larger portion of the magic wrap and that is exactly why the peacock's feathers are far more brightly coloured than those of the peahen and he has such a gorgeous tail. The peacock and peahen flew out of the house. They went to live among the other birds, now in the forest, now in the fields, looking for grain and tender green shoots to eat. The peacock remains our most beautiful bird. But he is always worried about his feathers. When storm clouds gather in the sky and thunder rumbles in the air, the peacock bursts into loud cries. People believe he does this because he is afraid the rain might spoil his gorgeous colours.

One into Two

This is a folk-tale from the state of Uttar Pradesh which is inhabited by many diverse races and people. In particular it has been a centre of Muslim culture for centuries. Among the Muslim families living in the towns and villages of the state 'Mian' and 'Begum' are popular forms of address for men and women. In Uttar Pradesh as in the rest of India, villagers are generally poor. So they like to weave fantasies like this one where the problem of poverty is solved by magic.

*

Kallu Mian and his wife Mumtaz lived in a village near the present day town of Barabanki. Their home was a mud-and-thatch hut atop a hill. Kallu was a shepherd. Every morning, winter or summer, he took his flocks to graze in the woods nearby. His sheep did well on the fresh green grass. Come shearing time, they gave him enough wool to make several blankets. Kallu sold the wool for good money and he and Mumtaz lived comfortably the whole year through.

But one year disaster struck. First one and then another and yet another of Kallu's sheep fell ill. Herbs and potions did not help. In a week's time the entire flock was dead. Kallu was shattered. He had no other means of earning a living. With his sheep gone, how would he and Mumtaz survive?

Weighed down by worry, Kallu spent many days sitting before his hut, a picture of despair. Shearing time came and went. The little money he had put by was soon gone. Every few days Kallu would go to town, sell some of his possessions, raise a little cash and buy some food. His shoes were worn down. Both he and Mumtaz were in need of new clothes. But where was the money?

One day, when Kallu was fretting his heart out over the loss of his sheep, Mumtaz had an idea. She called out from inside the hut, '*Ajee* (I say), can you hear me? Instead of moping around, why don't you do a bit of work? There's so much land around our hut. How about digging it up and planting a crop?'

The idea appealed to Kallu. But there was no spade in the house to dig with, for everything of value had been sold to buy food. Everything except a silver necklace that Mumtaz still wore around her neck. Now she took it off and gave it to Kallu saying, 'Take this and pawn it with the mahajan (moneylender). With the money buy some seeds and a bag of flour too. Meanwhile I shall go to the neighbours and borrow a spade.'

Kallu did as he was told. Upon returning home he fell to digging with all his might. The earth was bone dry and it took him all morning to dig up a small patch. But just as he was about to go in for his midday meal of dry chappatis and salt, his spade struck metal. CLANG! Hands trembling with excitement, Kallu began to clear the earth near the object. Finally he uncovered a large brass handi (vessel). The handi was empty. But as Kallu bent down to peep into it, his tobacco pouch slipped out of his pocket and fell in. Beside a few shreds of tobacco, the pouch contained five one rupee coins, left over from the money that the mahajan had given him for the necklace. Kallu saw the pouch fall but he did not give it a thought. Thrilled to bits, he yelled at the top of his voice, 'Begum, just come and see what I've found!'

Mumtaz came dashing out of the hut, still holding a pair of tongs, for she had been making chappatis. Her face lighted up when she saw the handi. 'Oh how wonderful!' she cried. 'We can sell that and buy some clothes for ourselves.' She bent forward to peep into the handi. As she did so, the tongs slipped from her hand and fell in. She put in a hand to take out the tongs, but in

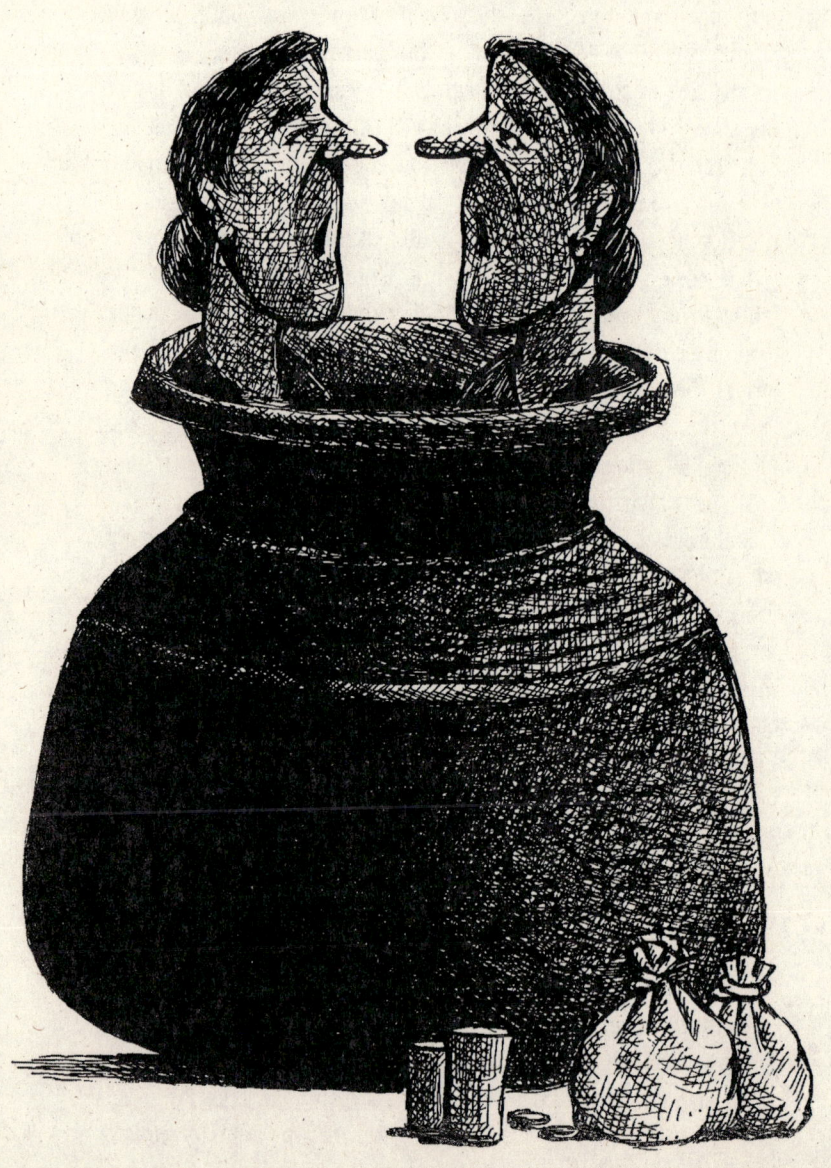

place of one pair she found two. She also found a second pouch containing, like the first, a few shreds of tobacco and five one rupee coins.

Mumtaz and Kallu stared at the things goggle-eyed. When the truth suddenly dawned on them, Kallu was all for grabbing Mumtaz and dancing a jig there and then. But Mumtaz had other ideas. She ran inside the hut and came back with an old and tattered blanket. This she stuffed inside the handi and took out two old and tattered blankets. Even the holes were identical in shape and size. Mumtaz was so excited she began to jump. 'At last I know how to get rich,' she cried, and went into action.

For a start, Mumtaz put in two tobacco pouches and took out four. Next she put in four and took out eight. Next she put in eight. . . Very soon they had a small pile of one rupee coins, to say nothing of the stack of pouches. Eyes shining with happiness, Mumtaz gave Kallu some of the money and said, 'Mian, go to the market at once and bring back the necklace you pawned. Get clothes for both of us and some sweets too. We must celebrate!'

Having packed off Kallu to the market, away went Mumtaz to the nearest neighbour to borrow a couple of potatoes. When Kallu came back, he found his wife perched on top of a mountain of potatoes and grinning from ear to ear. 'Come and see what I've brought you,' cried Kallu from afar. 'Your necklace is back too.' In her excitement Mumtaz slipped, rolled down the mountain of potatoes and whoosh! landed right inside the handi. Gallant as ever, Kallu ran to pull her out. But good heavens! There was another Mumtaz inside the handi, struggling to get out! Kallu went forward and helped her out too.

Mumtaz I stared at Mumtaz II in stunned silence and then she exploded. 'Why on earth did you have to pull her out?' she screamed at Kallu. 'What shall we do with her now?' So angry was she that she gave Kallu a mighty push and there, he also landed plonk inside the handi!

Now there was real trouble. Kallu I scrambled out of the handi, only to be followed immediately after by Kallu II. Mumtaz stared from one to other, utterly bewildered. But not for long, for she was a woman of ideas. 'I know what to do,' she cried happily. 'Let these two go and set up a separate house on the other side of the hill. That will be the best way to get rid of them.'

No sooner said than done. Kallu and Mumtaz helped the newcomers build a second hut of mud and thatch on the other side of the hill. When the hut was ready, Kallu and Mumtaz popped all their possessions into the handi, one by one. And the duplicates they handed over to the newcomers. So, in time, instead of one, there were two huts on the hill. And much to the amazement of the villagers, both huts were exactly alike in every detail, down to the couples who lived in them.

Tables Turned

Many Indian folk-tales are woven around the theme of justice. They uphold the view that a person wronged must get justice. Thus thieves, cheats and other wicked people should be punished and an honest person should get a reward or at least a compensation. But the justice shown in these stories is of a rough and ready kind. No legal discussions are involved. There are no lawyers. Instead, the judge catches the culprit by setting a simple trap.

'Tables Turned' is an old story from Tamil Nadu. It reflects the traditional marriage customs of that state and the importance enjoyed by elephants in olden times. The elephant is still very popular in Tamil Nadu and other parts of south India. It is a mount of choice on all special occasions. And flowers of course remain a must for the Tamil people.

*

In a town in Tamil Nadu there lived a potter. He had only one child, a son. The potter was by no means a rich man but he had great plans for his son. He spent good money on food and clothes for the boy and sent him to school. In due course the boy grew up to be a young man and was able to earn a living. It was time to get him married.

The potter looked at his son and his heart swelled with pride. 'I'll give him a grand wedding,' thought the potter, 'I'll get the best musicians, the best decorations, the best flowers and the best food that I can possibly afford. And after the ceremony is over, my son and his bride will be taken around the city in a grand procession. They won't go walking either, or in a hired carriage. They shall ride an elephant, like the children of wealthy landowners.'

In the same locality there lived an oil merchant who owned an elephant. This elephant he hired out to people on payment of a certain amount of money. The potter went to the oil merchant and took the elephant on hire for a day.

That night a grand procession was taken around the city. The bride and groom, dressed in all their finery, were seated on the elephant, which had been specially decorated for the occasion. They were followed by a happy, cheering crowd of men, women and children. Drummers and musicians walked alongside, playing on their instruments with gusto. In the middle of all this fun the elephant suddenly fell down and died.

The potter was shocked. The elephant had been fine. What happened to it all of a sudden? The potter kept thinking of the problem right through the night. Next morning he went to the oil merchant and said, 'I'm very sorry your elephant died suddenly while walking in the marriage procession. But don't worry. I shall pay you the full price of the elephant. Or, if you like, I can give you another elephant in return. Which shall it be?'

The oil merchant was a quarrelsome man by nature. He stood up and began to shout, 'What do you mean by offering me money or another elephant? I don't want either. I want my own elephant back. Did you hear me? Bring back the elephant I hired out to you or I shall lodge a complaint in court.' Naturally, the potter could not bring back the same elephant. So the oil merchant went and lodged a complaint against him in court.

The case came up for hearing. The judge asked the oil merchant, 'What is your complaint?'

'Justice, Your Honour, I want justice,' shouted the oil merchant. 'This man here borrowed my elephant and promised to return it the following day. But three days have passed and there is not a trace of that elephant. Your Honour, please order him to return my elephant.'

The judge turned to the potter and asked why he had not returned the elephant. The potter replied, 'Your Honour, what this man says is correct. I did borrow the elephant, promising to return it the following day. The elephant was being taken in procession, with the bride and groom seated on it, when it suddenly dropped dead. How can I possibly return it when it is dead? And how am I to blame for the mishap? I offered to pay for the elephant or to buy another one in its place. But the oil merchant turned down the offer. All he wants is his own elephant back.'

The judge thought that the offer was very fair indeed. He tried to reason with the oil merchant. But the fellow flatly refused to listen. 'It's my elephant and I want nothing but my elephant,' he said. 'The potter agreed to return it in a day. Make him do it, Your Honour.'

The judge was a wise man. He saw that it was no use arguing with the oil merchant. So he postponed the hearing till the following day. When the oil merchant had left, the judge called the potter and told him, 'I can see that you're an honest man. You are also making a very fair offer. So I shall help you. Now listen.' And the judge whispered something in the potter's ear. The potter nodded and went away smiling.

When court re-opened the following morning there was no trace of the potter. The oil merchant was hopping up and down complaining, 'See, he has run away. Didn't I tell you, Your Honour, that that man is a swindler?'

After waiting impatiently for some more time the oil merchant said to the judge, 'Your Honour, I have a feeling that the potter is hiding inside his house. He is scared to come here. Have I your permission to go and bring him personally?' The judge agreed at once and ordered a junior court officer to accompany the oil merchant.

They reached the potter's house and the oil merchant knocked at the door. Good and hard. There was no reply. He hammered at the door with his fists and called out the potter's name at the top of his lungs. But there was dead silence within. The oil merchant lost his temper. 'Hide from me, will you?' he yelled. 'I'll show you!' And with that he gave the door a mighty push. Little did he know that the potter had stacked a whole lot of earthen pots against the door. With the push they all came crashing to the floor. And that very minute the potter came charging out of the back door crying aloud, 'Oh my pots, my beautiful pots! What have you gone and done? You have destroyed all the precious pots that my ancestors had left me. I shall go to the judge immediately and complain against you!'

When they came before the judge, the oil merchant offered to pay for the pots or to replace them. But the potter turned up his nose at the offer. 'Nothing doing, I want my own pots back,' he declared. 'My ancestors gave them to me. They were the pride and glory of my house. What will I do with the money or a whole lot of brand new pots? This man has broken my pots, Your Honour. Make him give them back to me.'

Now the oil merchant was in a fix. How could he make the broken pots whole again? In the end he said, 'Your Honour, if this man drops his demand for those old pots, I shall not ask for my elephant back.'

The potter pretended to be unwilling. But finally he accepted the offer and the case was settled. Thus the quarrelsome oil merchant lost on both counts. He lost an elephant and got no money either. Even the potter lost a few pots. But they were not of so much value. In a week's time he had made a whole lot of new ones to replace them.

Work for the Demon

This is a story from the Punjab, a state known for its fertile land and prosperous farmers. This story shows that in some cases prosperity can make people greedy and get them into serious trouble. It also shows that sometimes, when a man is in trouble, it takes a woman to rescue him. The woman helps him out not by a show of strength but by using her head.

*

Once there lived a man called Sher Dil. He was a rich man with acres of farmland and so many heads of cattle he didn't know what to do with them. All that land and all those heads of cattle made for a lot of work. So Sher Dil had engaged a hundred servants to work for him. But Sher Dil was at heart a miser. He hated to spend money feeding the servants and paying their wages.

Sher Dil's wife Gulabo was his exact opposite in temperament. She was patient and good natured and very wise. Whenever Sher Dil grumbled about expenses, she rebuked him saying, 'Our servants work for us all day long, right round the year. So what if they cost money? We still have more than enough. Why can't you be grateful for all that the great Lord has given us?' But her words of wisdom had no effect whatsoever on her ill tempered, miserly husband.

One day Sher Dil sat down to do his accounts and sure enough, he soon started grumbling. 'Just look at these figures. Why do servants have to eat so much? Why can't I find *one* slave who will handle all the jobs alone?'

'What? Are you crazy?' said Gulabo. 'How can a single human being possibly handle all that work? Perhaps you're thinking of employing a demon!'

Sher Dil sat up. 'And why not?' cried he, suddenly very excited. 'One demon can easily do the work of a hundred ordinary servants. And he doesn't have to be fed at all. I'm told demons catch their own food from the forest!' The more he thought over this idea, the more he liked it. And Sher Dil made up his mind to visit a sadhu who granted boons to people and put an end to their troubles.

It took Sher Dil two days to reach the sadhu's hut, situated in the middle of a forest. The sadhu sat deep in meditation. At long last he opened his eyes and asked Sher Dil what he had come for. Sher Dil bowed his head. 'Maharaj,' he said, 'I'm greatly troubled by the team of servants who work on my farm. They are eating me out of house and home. They cost so much that I shall soon become a pauper. Pray grant me a demon who can be my slave and do all the work single-handed.'

'So be it,' replied the sadhu. He picked up a stick, closed his eyes and murmured something. Then he drove the stick into the ground. Next minute a thin stream of smoke began to emerge from the top end of the stick. Slowly the stream increased in volume till it became a small cloud, rumbling like thunder. And out of the cloud stepped a huge, blue-coloured demon as tall as a pipal tree. He looked so fierce that Sher Dil felt like running away. But somehow he stood his ground. The demon roared, 'Why have I been summoned, master?'

'To serve this gentleman,' replied the sadhu.

'But master,' roared the demon again, 'does he know my terms of employment? Please tell him that he must keep me busy from sunrise to sunrise. The moment I find there's no work for me, I'll eat him up.'

Sher Dil burst out laughing. 'You won't get a chance, there'll be so much work to do on the farm. You'll milk the cattle, take them out to graze and bring in fodder for them. You'll plough the land, sow the seed, weed and water the crop and make sure the parrots don't damage it. When the grain is ripe you must harvest it, sell it in the market, bring me the money and then get down to digging the land again. How does that sound, eh? Is it work enough for you?'

'We'll see, we'll see,' said the demon with a frown. 'What do I do now?'

'Take me home,' said Sher Dil.

The words were hardly out of his mouth when the demon snatched him up, tucked him behind one ear and went flying across the sky. Afraid of rolling off, Sher Dil clutched the demon's ear with both hands and peeped over it. The earth appeared like a tiny multicoloured ball. Sher Dil closed his eyes for fear. Then suddenly the demon began to descend like an egg thrown up in the air. He touched down at Sher Dil's own doorstep. Sher Dil scrambled off and ran to see his wife. 'Look what I've found,' he cried, bursting with excitement. 'A real demon to do all our work. You can't imagine how tough he is. It took me two days to reach the sadhu's hut but the demon brought me back in five minutes flat!'

Before his wife could say anything in reply, Sher Dil had sacked all his servants and sent off the demon to plough the land. Then he yawned, stretched himself and lay down on his bed for a nice little nap.

Sher Dil was in the middle of a rosy dream when someone grabbed him by the shoulder and shook him hard. 'Huh, uh,' muttered Sher Dil as he sat up. The demon stood towering over him. 'Wake up, master,' he said impatiently. 'The fields have been ploughed. What shall I do now?'

Sher Dil could not believe his ears. So many acres of land, ploughed up in less than a quarter of an hour! He climbed to his roof and looked around. To be sure, the land had been ploughed as far as the eye could see.

'Go, get some manure and mix it with the soil,' Sher Dil ordered the demon. 'When you have finished, sow the seed and water the fields.'

The demon disappeared and Sher Dil went back to sleep again. But he had barely snored a couple of times when someone shook him again, harder than before. 'Master,' said the demon's voice, 'the work is done. What shall I do now?'

By this time Sher Dil was quite irritated. 'Why don't you let me sleep? Go and raise a fence all around my land,' he ordered. The demon left but Sher Dil did not go back to sleep again. From his kitchen window he watched the demon fetch a pile of wood and some tools. His hands flew as one stick after another was cut and shaped and driven into the ground. Before Sher Dil had finished his evening cup of tea the demon was back again. 'The fence is ready, master. What shall I do now?'

Sher Dil sent him off to empty out their pond and fill it with fresh water from the river. Night was falling when the demon returned to say that the work had been done. 'What shall I do now?' he asked.

'Why don't you rest a little?' said Sher Dil in despair. The demon laughed, a horrible, croaky laugh. 'Oh, I never rest,' he thundered. 'For me it's only work, work and work.'

Sher Dil picked up courage enough to say, 'Well, I want to rest till sunrise tomorrow morning.'

'And what shall I do till then?' demanded the demon, rolling his eyes.

'Guard the fields so no wild animal can get in and trample down the seed.'

The demon went away but Sher Dil could not sleep a wink. Just before dawn he woke up his wife and said tearfully, 'What on earth shall I do now? If this demon doesn't get work to do, he'll eat me up. And I'm fast running out of work. The only thing that I can possibly ask him to do now is to build a new house for us. But that will be done in half an hour. And then . . . ? Oh dear, it was so much better with a hundred servants, even if they cost a lot. Why did I act such a miser?'

Gulabo comforted him. 'Just leave everything to me,' she said. 'You go right back to sleep.'

As soon as the sun peeped over the horizon, the demon began to hammer at the door. 'Work,' he yelled. 'Give me some work to do, master, or I'll eat you up.'

Gulabo opened the door a crack and peeped out. 'Shhh! Keep quiet,' she said, a finger on her lips. 'Don't you know your master's asleep?'

'Huh!' snorted the demon. 'Give me some work this minute or that will be the end of both of you!'

Gulabo came out of the door. 'Don't worry,' she said in a soothing tone. 'He'll wake soon enough. In the meantime, will you do a small job for me?' Just outside the door stood a stray dog that often came there looking for food. Gulabo told the demon, 'I think that dog would look much better if its tail were straight and not curled. Will you please straighten its tail for me?'

The demon bent down, caught the dog's tail by the tip and gave it a good jerk. The tail straightened out. But the moment he let go, it curled up again. The demon caught the tail a second time and stroked it for a good five minutes. 'There,' he said finally. 'That should do the trick.' But the moment he let go, the tail curled up again. With a frown on his face the demon caught the tail for the third time, rolled it up the other way and held it in position for some time, But the moment he let go, the tail curled up again, back to its original shape.

All this time the dog had been watching patiently as the demon fiddled around with its tail. But suddenly it lost its patience. With a bound it was up and barking at the demon. Round and round they went, the demon dodging and ducking and diving at the tail and the dog snapping and snarling and threatening to bite. This went on for hours. In the end the demon got fed up of trying to catch the dog. 'I just can't do it,' he said. But he was thoroughly ashamed of himself at the same time. 'I failed to straighten that dog's tail. How can I possibly show my face in that house again?' And off he went to hide in the forest that he came from.

With the demon gone, Sher Dil and his wife began to live in peace once again. Sher Dil took back all his servants and gave them a solid feed to start with. And never, never again did he complain about the amount that he had to spend on their food and wages.

The Qazi of Jaunpur

This is a story from Uttar Pradesh. Many of the characters here are still commonly seen in the villages and towns of Uttar Pradesh. There are learned men known as Maulvi Sahibs still working as teachers. They are held in great respect, particularly by the people who are uneducated themselves. True, the qazi has been replaced by the magistrate. But labourers like Jumman are a common sight. And an ass is still a popular beast of burden all over the state.

*

Once there was a Maulvi Sahib. He lived in a village and was a master at the village school, which had but a single room and a handful of students, all boys. But a master is a master and Maulvi Sahib was a very important man. The villagers thought the world of him and asked him for guidance whenever they had a problem. As a result Maulvi Sahib was all puffed up with pride. He always carried a cane in his hand and swung it around as he walked down the village street. 'There's no better teacher in the world than I,' he used to say, his nose in the air. 'Why, I can make a man out of an ass!'

He said this so many times that he soon began to believe it himself. If anybody tried to argue a point with him, Maulvi Sahib would retort, 'You'd better agree with me. I'm no ordinary person. Don't you know, I can turn an ass into a man?'

One day Maulvi Sahib lost his temper with one of his students. He caught the boy by the ear and gave him a good whacking.

'Out of my sight, dunce!' yelled Maulvi Sahib. 'I never saw a more stupid fellow. My very touch has turned so many asses into men. But you? You'll always remain an ass. . .!'

At that very moment a man called Jumman was passing by the schoolroom window. Jumman was a labourer. He earned a living by carrying loads for other people—bricks, bags of wheat and rice, vegetables from the fields. To carry these loads he made use of an ass. Now this ass was so useless, he gave his master a headache almost every day. He was slow and stubborn and totally unwilling to work. Jumman was a simple man. The moment he heard Maulvi Sahib say that his very touch had turned asses into men, Jumman thought, 'Why don't I bring that worthless ass of mine to Maulvi Sahib? Maybe he can turn the creature into a man too. Wouldn't that be simply wonderful? Then my ass will work for me like a son. He will earn and my wife and I will sit back and enjoy life!'

The more he thought about it, the more he liked the idea. He hurried home to fetch his ass.

Jumman put a rope around his ass's neck and drove it to school. Maulvi Sahib was still busy making his pupils repeat the Urdu alphabet, 'alif, bey, pey. . .' Jumman waited patiently under a tree till the last student had left and Maulvi Sahib rose to go home. Then he ran to the door and fell at Maulvi Sahib's feet. 'Huzoor,' cried Jumman, 'I've come with great hopes. Don't disappoint me please. I'm a poor man.'

'What's all this about?' said Maulvi Sahib with a frown. 'What on earth do you want?'

'Janaab,' said Jumman, 'I have an ass.'

'So?' cut in Maulvi Sahib with some annoyance.

'Huzoor, he's such an ass he doesn't listen to me at all.'

'An ass has got to be an ass,' replied Maulvi Sahib. 'He can't be a man.'

'Oh, but he can: Only this morning I heard you say that your very touch has turned many asses into men!'

Suddenly Maulvi Sahib realized what had happened. But he wasn't going to tell Jumman the truth. Instead he put on a stern face. 'Yes yes, I can turn an ass into a man all right. But what has that got to do with you?'

Once again Jumman fell at Maulvi Sahib's feet. 'Huzoor, take pity on me. Turn my ass into a man, I beg of you. Maybe then he'll listen to me. . . .'

Maulvi Sahib realized that this was his chance of making a little extra money. Aloud he said, 'What a dimwit you are! Is it such a simple thing to turn an ass into a man? It is hard work and it costs money. I must prepare a special masala which takes a week to grind.'

'Please, please be so kind as to prepare that masala for me,' begged Jumman. 'I'm willing to pay for it.'

'A hundred rupees?'

Jumman hesitated a bit.

'Make up your mind fast,' said Maulvi Sahib. 'I don't have much time. After all, a hundred rupees isn't much to pay for turning a worthless ass into a smart young man.'

Jumman gave in. He drove his ass to Maulvi Sahib's house, tied it to a stake in the courtyard and ran home again to fetch the money. As he placed the money in Maulvi Sahib's palm, he asked in all humility, 'How long will it take to turn my ass into a man?' Maulvi Sahib thought a bit. 'Ten days,' he said. 'No. It seems like a difficult case. Make it twelve.'

'I'll come after a fortnight,' said Jumman. He bent almost double to salaam Maulvi Sahib. Then singing aloud for sheer happiness he went back home.

Maulvi Sahib waited a couple of days just in case Jumman changed his mind. Then he sold the ass for fifty rupees. He bought himself some new clothes and shoes. And with the rest of the money he and his wife feasted on kofta and biryani for a whole week.

Meanwhile Jumman could hardly sleep for excitement. He made all sorts of plans. When his ass became a man, how much would he earn? What comforts would they buy? New quilts? A new trunk for keeping clothes? A goat to give them milk?

At the end of a fortnight, on the dot, Jumman was back. Maulvi Sahib was looking much fatter and happier than before. He wasn't even shouting at the children. Jumman waited patiently for the last student to leave, and then ran to Maulvi Sahib. 'Salaam Huzoor,' he said. 'Is the job done?'

With the extra money Maulvi Sahib was so comfortable that he had almost forgotten Jumman. It took him a minute to recognize the man. 'Oh ah,' he said. 'Yes of course. You left your ass with me.'

'Janaab. And I paid good money for the ass to be changed into a man,' Jumman reminded him anxiously.

Maulvi Sahib nodded. 'You did, you did,' he beamed at Jumman. 'And the job has been done!'

'Has it indeed?' Jumman leapt with excitement. 'Where's my a—my son? Tell me quick so I can meet him.'

Maulvi Sahib threw up his hands. 'To meet him you must go to Jaunpur. You see, by mistake I put too much "masala" on the tail. So the ass not only became a man, he turned into the Qazi (magistrate) of Jaunpur!'

Jumman couldn't believe his ears. The Qazi of Jaunpur! *His* ass? His *own* worthless, good for nothing, stubborn, nitwit of an ass? Had he really become the Qazi of Jaunpur? An officer so important? So highly respected?

When the information had finally sunk in, Jumman was a changed man. Gone was the humble manner, the deep salaams, the habit of going down on his knees before others. He drew himself up to his full height and announced, 'I'm going to Jaunpur today!' And turning on his heel, he marched down the village street.

Jumman reached Jaunpur the following day, all dusty and tired from travelling. He had a wash at a wayside tank, took off his turban, smoothed down his hair and tied the turban back in position. He ran his finger through his beard and dusted his clothes. After all, he was going to meet an officer. Never mind if that officer was only an ass to begin with. Now he was a man and a very important man at that!

At first the city baffled Jumman. But at last he found his way to the Qazi's court. He pushed his way past the guards at the gate and marched straight in. The Qazi was busy settling a dispute between two shopkeepers. Jumman went and stood squarely in front of the Qazi. 'Adabarz janaab,' he said in a slightly mocking tone, 'how does it feel to be changed from an ass into a man? Great, isn't it?'

A sudden hush fell over the court. The Qazi's face slowly turned a deep red. 'Who is this man?' he demanded angrily. 'Turn him out, someone.'

The guards ran to catch hold of Jumman. But he shook them off and faced the Qazi again. 'Oh, so now you don't even recognize me, is it? You've grown too big for your old master? And it was only yesterday that I fed you with fresh green grass! How easily people forget a kindness done to them!'

The Qazi rose to his feet and thundered, 'Throw this man out!'

But Jumman was too nimble for the guards. He jumped on to a table and said aloud, 'You always were a lazy, good-for-nothing creature. Don't I know you? So what if you've become a man? You remain an ass . . .'

At this point one of the guards caught hold of Jumman. 'Put him in the lockup for the night,' said the Qazi. 'That will bring him to his senses.'

Jumman spent the night in the lockup but it did not help matters. Next day he was back again at the court of the Qazi. 'So you'll have me locked up, is it?' he cried. 'Your own master, who bought you for as much as forty rupees at a fair? You deserved to remain an ass. Oh, why did I pay good money to have you changed into a man?'

By now the Qazi was certain that Jumman was out of his mind. He thought it best to humour the man. 'Look here,' he told Jumman, 'I've had enough of this. What is it that you want?'

'Five hundred rupees,' said Jumman promptly. The Qazi gave him a bag and said, 'Here's the money. Take it and leave the court this minute. Remember, if you come again, you'll spend the rest of your life in jail!'

Jumman took the money and went back to his village. With the money he bought himself another ass. He also bought a goat, a new trunk and two quilts. Thanks to the Qazi of Jaunpur, Jumman and his wife spent the rest of their days in comfort.

The Secret Valley

This is a folk-tale told by the Lepcha tribe of Sikkim. The Lepchas are a people who came to inhabit Sikkim a long time ago. They settled down on the slopes of the great peak Kanchenjunga. The Lepchas call themselves Rong, which in their language means 'the people of the valley'.

Like all tribal people of the world, the Lepchas love stories. In winter they gather around a fire and tell stories about a variety of topics — the creation of the world, the origin of the Lepcha people, the seasons and other natural phenomena and, of course, ghosts and demons. This story is very old. It comes from the Lepchas who originally settled in Sikkim and has been handed down by word of mouth from one generation to another.

*

The Lepcha people live on the slopes of the great Kanchenjunga and look upon the peak with great awe. They believe that Kanchenjunga is the home of gods and spirits and therefore sacred. They also believe that, high up in the mountains behind the Kanchenjunga, there is a secret valley called Mayel. And in this valley live the ancestors of the Lepcha tribe. Hundreds of years have passed but these elders are still believed to be living at Mayel. And nobody can go there, for the way to Mayel is guarded by ferocious demons who will not let anyone through. Besides, the passage is blocked by a huge stone which cannot be removed by any man.

At one time these elders used to come down to the valley where the Lepchas live now. They mixed with the people and shared in their joys and sorrows. But they no longer do so because

they feel that the new generations of Lepchas are not as good and pious as they should be. When the elders stopped coming, the Lepchas of the valley were very sad. They kept looking for their elders. For hundreds of years they looked but never found what they were looking for.

One day a brave young Lepcha was hunting in a remote forest when he came upon a stream. Floating down the stream was the branch of a tree. Instead of leaves it had beautiful blue-green needles, and the bark looked as though it was made of gold. The young man knew that there was no such tree growing in the valley. 'This branch must have come from Mayel,' thought he. 'And that means Mayel must lie somewhere upstream.'

Leaving his bag of game on the forest floor and forgetting all about hunting, the young Lepcha began to climb up the mountain. He followed the path of the stream. So excited was he that he climbed for days and days but never got tired. In time he crossed the forest and a range of snow-covered mountains. After several more days he came to an open space at the heart of which lay a lake. Around the lake the young Lepcha saw a whole lot of white feathers. 'I wonder which birds shed these feathers?' thought he. 'I can't see any birds around.'

He pressed on and then, at long last, he reached a lush green valley surrounded by tall mountains. This was Mayel, the home of the Lepchas' ancestors.

The sun was already setting when the young man reached the first house in the valley. He knocked at the stout wooden door and an old woman opened it. She took him in and offered him a rug to sit on. Then she brought him some hot water to wash his feet. Later, when he was rested, she served a simple but satisfying meal of roasted grain, fruit and milk. The old woman was soon joined by an old man and the young Lepcha learned that the old couple lived all by themselves in that house. 'Have you no children?' asked the young man. 'No, we don't,' replied the old couple.

The young Lepcha lay down on the rug and was soon fast asleep. He slept soundly till the sun rose again behind the mountain peaks. And then he was awakened by the sound of children at play. He got out of bed to find a little boy and girl running about the house. He thought they must be the neighbours' children and the old people had probably gone to work in the fields. But when he asked the children who they were, they laughed merrily. 'We are the old couple you met last evening,' they said.

'How is that possible?' asked the young man, thoroughly confused.

'That is the way our world goes,' the children informed him. 'In the morning we are children. By midday we grow up into adults. In the evening we are old. But by the following morning we become children again. In this way we live on for ever.'

The young Lepcha spent seven very happy days in the valley. He roamed around, enjoying the beautiful scenery. He saw a whole forest of trees with blue-green needles and golden bark. And morning and evening he saw large flocks of white birds winging their way across the sky.

At the end of seven days the old woman told the young Lepcha, 'Son, now you must go back where you came from, for no ordinary human is allowed to live in Mayel. But wait a minute. I have a gift for you.'

The old woman gave him the seeds of several different kinds of grain. She said, 'Sow these seeds in your village and your people will always have plenty to eat. But remember to sow them at the proper time or they will not grow.'

The young man asked, 'How will I know which is the proper time?'

Just then a flock of white birds flew past them. The old woman smiled. 'We shall send you these birds as messengers. When you see a flock of white birds in your village, know that it is time to get down to work in the fields.'

The Lepchas believe that this is how they came to have foodgrains. To this day when they see flocks of white birds, they know it is time for them to sow their crops. Once the sowing is over, they begin to pray to their ancestors in Mayel to send them a good harvest.

Enter Mulla Do-Piaza

It is a strange fact of history that Akbar, the greatest Mughal emperor, was illiterate. At the time of Akbar's birth and for many years after, his father Humayun was a fugitive. Having lost his kingdom to the Afghan Sher Shah Suri, Humayun was constantly moving from place to place seeking shelter. He was too unsettled to think of educating his son and that is why Akbar came to the throne without having received a formal education. But perhaps this was why Akbar valued learned men so highly. He honoured them with money and titles and positions at court. Educated men from all over the empire flocked to Agra, Akbar's capital, in the hope of finding favour with the emperor. Here is the story of one such man. He is popularly known as Mulla Do-Piaza because he invented a dish known as do-piaza. Do-Piaza is made with mutton and double its quantity of onions.

*

Mulla Do-Piaza was the son of humble parents. His father was a schoolmaster. There was never much money in the house so Mulla Do-Piaza never enjoyed any luxuries. All he wanted was to learn more and more. Books were not so easily available then as they are now. They were handwritten and very expensive. Mulla Do-Piaza read all the books that he could lay his hands on. Sometimes he went to a rich man's house and took up a petty job just so that he could read the books in that house.

In due course he had mastered Persian and Arabic, philosophy and astronomy. And now Mulla Do-Piaza was not content to stay at home. He began to dream of going to Agra and getting a position at the court of Akbar.

It was very difficult to get a position at court. One really had to excel in some field. Also, one needed a patron, that is, a man who was already a courtier and close enough to the emperor to recommend a newcomer. It was months before Mulla Do-Piaza could find a patron and months before the patron could find a suitable opportunity to recommend him to the emperor. Akbar asked for details of Mulla Do-Piaza's life — where he lived, what he had learnt, and what kind of work he could do. On hearing that Mulla Do-Piaza was well versed in Persian and Arabic, philosophy and astronomy, Akbar was quiet for a while. Then he said, 'Very well, we are pleased to give this young man a chance. Let him take charge of the royal murghikhana (poultry house).'

When Mulla Do-Piaza got the news he was heartbroken. What? In charge of the royal murghikhana? He, a scholar, capable of debating with the most learned men in the empire, had been asked to look after a few hundred brainless, clucking hens? What an insult to him! What an insult to all the time he had spent poring over books, day after day, night after night!

But Mulla Do-Piaza was basically a patient man. He knew that to get good things in life one must work hard and wait. So he got down to work with great determination. From sun up to sun down his only concern was hens, hens, hens. He saw to it that they were well fed and given clean water to drink. He saw to it that their living quarters were clean. And if a fowl was taken ill, he made sure that it was immediately separated from the rest and given proper treatment.

After a day's hard work among the hens, Mulla Do-Piaza still sat down with his books. Now and again he heaved a deep sigh. 'When, oh when will the emperor admit me to court?' he cried.

Meanwhile Akbar had forgotten all about the scholar whom he had packed off to mind the hens. But one day he remembered. His finance minister, Raja Todar Mal, was reading out the palace accounts to tell Akbar how much money had been spent on the royal household. When the minister came to the expenses of the murghikhana, he mentioned such a low figure that Akbar sat up. 'How is that?' he demanded. 'Why are we spending so little on our hens? Have most of them died or what?'

The minister bowed very low. 'No, Your Majesty, I was there this morning. The hens are not only alive, they're looking very plump and fit. That young scholar is looking after them.'

'Send for him,' ordered Akbar.

Mulla Do-Piaza came as fast as he could. Akbar looked at him sternly. 'Why are you spending so little on our hens? Aren't you feeding them properly?'

Mulla Do-Piaza replied, 'Jahanpanah (a royal title, meaning 'the refuge of the world'), your humble servant is feeding them very well. Only the food is different.'

'What do you mean?'

'Jahanpanah, I'm feeding them what cannot be used in the royal kitchen. Vegetable stalks, fruit and vegetable peelings, stale chappatis and dough used for sealing the mouths of vessels when royal cooks prepare special dishes for Your Majesty. All this is waste. Normally it is thrown away. But hens not only enjoy it, they thrive on it. It is very good for them.'

Akbar nodded. 'Hm, that was good work, young man. We hereby promote you to the rank of royal librarian.'

Mulla Do-Piaza salaamed the emperor a dozen times. But in his heart of hearts he was bitterly disappointed. He had spent the first thirty years of his life gaining knowledge. Now he wished to air that knowledge. He wished to show people how clever he was. But as head of the royal library he would be seeing only books and more books and very few people.

In time, however, Mulla Do-Piaza got over his disappointment. He buckled down to work organizing the library. One day, about an year later, Akbar came to inspect the library. He was surprised to find each book covered with a jacket of silk, velvet or brocade. There were hundreds of books and not one without a cover. Akbar sent for Mulla Do-Piaza again. 'You have used very expensive material to cover these books,' he said. 'But you have never charged us for it. Surely you're not spending your own money to cover the books in the royal library!'

Mulla Do-Piaza bowed. 'Jahanpanah, those covers did not cost anything.'

'Impossible!' said the emperor. 'We don't believe you.'

'Indeed, Your Majesty, I got them absolutely free of cost. Every day dozens of people come to the Diwan-e-Aam (Hall of Public Audience) with humble requests to Your Majesty. These requests are written on sheets of paper. The paper is folded and placed inside a bag made of the most expensive material that the person can afford—either silk, velvet or brocade. Your Majesty's ministers take out the paper so the request may reach Your Majesty's august ears. But the bags are discarded.

'I saw hundreds of such bags lying in a store behind the Diwan-e-Aam. The royal tailors soon made them into jackets for the books. Since these tailors are already in Your Majesty's service, they charged me nothing.'

Akbar looked at Mulla Do-Piaza and smiled broadly. 'Young man, you have proved yourself worthy of great things. From tomorrow you shall be one of our courtiers.' And that is how, through patience and hard work, Mulla Do-Piaza finally got his heart's desire.

The Ghost That Got Away

The home of this story, Kangra, is a district of Himachal. It is a hilly area and the people are simple. In rural Kangra, as in other parts of India, a young man feels shy and awkward when going to his in-laws' place for the first time. The story is woven around just such a situation. It has a universal appeal because it could have happened anywhere.

*

In a village in Kangra there lived a young man named Dhania. He owned a small grocery shop and made a comfortable living for himself. But he was basically a simpleton. Even the smallest day-to-day problems made him nervous. And when he was nervous, he ran to his friend Kulfi Ram for guidance. Kulfi Ram was a fortune-teller. Every day he sat under a mango tree, waiting for people to come along and ask him to read their palms.

One day, as Kulfi Ram sat under the tree, Dhania came running. He looked more nervous than ever. At the sight of him Kulfi Ram laughed. 'There you are again,' he said. 'What great calamity has befallen you this time? Has a customer asked for four annas worth of rice on credit?' And Kulfi Ram laughed some more.

'Oh, stop making fun of me,' cried Dhania. 'This time it's serious.'

'Oh really?' said Kulfi Ram. 'Come, let's go to the teashop.' A little later the two friends were sipping tea from small glass tumblers. 'Tell me all,' said Kulfi Ram.

'I - I,' stammered Dhania, 'I have to go to my father-in-law's place.'

'What?' laughed Kulfi Ram. 'Is that all? Then you should be happy. You'll have a jolly good time. Everyone in your wife's family will be running around, trying to make you comfortable. You'll get delicious food to eat. . .'

'That's all very well,' broke in Dhania. 'But this is the first time I'm going to my in-laws' place after marriage. Worse, since I'm going on business, my wife will not be accompanying me.'

'So?'

Dhania lost his patience. 'You know very well I don't wish to go. What will I do there? What will I say to them? I'm scared.'

Kulfi Ram pumped his hand good and hard. 'Leave it to me, my friend. I'll tell you exactly what to do and what to say.'

'Why don't you come with me? Then you can guide me at every step,' Dhania asked him.

Kulfi Ram liked the idea very much and the very next day the two men set out. On the way Kulfi Ram told Dhania, 'Two things you must remember. Don't talk too much and don't eat too much. Your in-laws must not say, "My, what a chatterbox" or "Goodness, what a glutton"!'

In a few hours they arrived at their destination. The whole family turned out to welcome them. Dhania's mother-in-law greeted them with folded hands. 'Welcome *Jwai Ji* (son-in-law). How fortunate we are to have you come to our place.'

Dhania was slowly turning red in the face but Kulfi Ram had told him not to talk too much. So he returned his in-laws' greeting with folded hands but said not a word. Kulfi Ram spoke instead, 'My friend is rather tired after a long journey. He would like to go to bed early.'

'Yes yes, of course,' said Dhania's mother-in-law. 'Dinner is ready. I'll serve it at once.' The guests were led to the kitchen. They were asked to sit on a thick straw mat spread on the floor. Dhania's eyes almost popped out of his head to see the food, particularly the crisp, golden pooris. He ate two at one go when suddenly he remembered Kulfi Ram's words, 'Don't eat too much.' He simply had to follow his friend's advice. So, after the second poori, he refused everything else that was offered. It broke his heart but he kept saying 'No, no, no.' Meanwhile Kulfi Ram was eating away steadily, enjoying every morsel. 'My friend is a small eater,' he said between mouthfuls. 'Indeed he is,' said Dhania's father-in-law. 'Quite remarkable! He's so young and he eats so little!'

After the meal was over, the two friends found themselves in a room with two beds. The mattresses were so comfortable that the moment they lay down, they fell asleep.

But in the middle of the night Dhania woke up. His stomach was making the queerest sounds, rumbling and gurgling. It could mean only one thing. He was hungry. Dhania lay still for some time, hoping he would fall asleep, but he soon realized it was hopeless. With each passing moment he got hungrier and hungrier. At length he could stand it no more. He shook his friend by the arm and whispered, 'Wake up Kulfi! I'm hungry.'

'Hungry?' snapped Kulfi Ram, sitting up. 'You've no business to be hungry after that lavish dinner.'

'Lavish dinner?' said Dhania crossly. 'Didn't you tell me not to eat too much? Now get up and do something about it.'

'Oh all right,' muttered Kulfi Ram as he rolled out of bed. He opened the door and peeped out. Their room overlooked a courtyard. On the other side of the courtyard was a room which was probably the store, because they had seen the lady of the house go in and come out with a tin of ghee. The store was sure to have something to eat. But it also had a lock on the door. Kulfi Ram thought for a while and said, 'Dhania, I can't possibly provide you with food at this hour, unless we wake up your mother-in-law and ask her for some leftover pooris.'

'No no no no,' begged Dhania in panic. 'For heaven's sake! I will never be able to show her my face again.'

'All right, all right,' said Kulfi Ram soothingly. 'In that case you must sneak into the store and look around. With luck you'll find something to eat.'

'How do I get into the store?'

'There's a skylight just wide enough to admit you. And there's a rope in that corner, used for tethering cattle. You can tie the rope around your waist, climb up on my shoulders and scramble in through the skylight. I'll be standing outside. When you've eaten your fill, call out my name and I'll haul you up.'

A few minutes later Dhania was inside the store. At first he couldn't see a thing. But slowly, as his eyes got used to the dark, he could make out some shapes—boxes, tins, bottles and buckets. There were sacks of rice and wheat but nothing, alas, that he could eat. And then Dhania caught sight of an earthen pitcher hanging from the roof. His heart leapt up. 'Now this must be either milk or butter or curd. Something ready to eat. And my mother-in-law must have hung it up there so the cat can't get it. But I'll get it all right.'

Dhania stood up on a box and stretched out one arm as far as it would go. But he barely managed to touch the bottom of the pitcher. 'Huh!' said Dhania, getting quite desperate. He picked up a stick standing in a corner and gave the pitcher a smart tap. There was a cracking sound and a thin stream of something began to flow out of the pitcher. Dhania eagerly opened his mouth to catch the stream, took a big gulp and realized it was honey.

For a few minutes Dhania stood under the pitcher and drank his fill of honey. But suddenly, without warning, a large chunk of the pitcher broke away and the thin stream became a torrent. Before Dhania had time to get out of the way, he was covered with honey. It was all over his hair. It got into his eyes and ears and ran down his nose into his kurta. He tried to get away but there was honey under his feet and he was stuck to the floor. 'Kulfi Ram!' yelled Dhania, 'pull me out!'

'Shhhh!' said Kulfi Ram from outside. 'Not so loud. Have you gone mad? I'll pull you out.'

But this was easier said than done. Kulfi Ram was a thin, scrawny fellow and Dhania was no lightweight. Besides, the honey under Dhania's feet held him fast. Kulfi Ram pulled for all he was worth. But he barely managed to lift Dhania a couple of feet off the ground before he ran out of breath. And back went Dhania with a thud.

And so it went on, ding-dong, ding-dong, ding-dong, till Dhania could take no more. 'Kulfi Ram!' he yelled again, 'pull me out this minute!' The noise woke up Dhania's father-in-law and he came running. 'What's happened?' he whispered. At the very sight of him Kulfi Ram's heart sank. But he was a quick-witted man. 'Not to worry Bauji,' he smiled back. 'This is an old story.'

'What old story?' returned Dhania's father-in-law. 'I must know.'

Kulfi Ram threw up one hand in despair. 'Bauji' he said, 'what can I do? For the last five years a ghost has been after my life. He wants me to go with him on a pilgrimage. But tell me Bauji, can a man in his senses go on a pilgrimage with a ghost, of all things?'

'Never!' said Dhania's father-in-law with feeling. 'What a ridiculous idea!'

'Exactly,' said Kulfi Ram. 'The ghost has even followed me to your place. Somehow I managed to push him into the store and keep him there. But I'm wondering how to get rid of him.'

'Please, please get rid of him fast,' begged Dhania's father-in-law. He had been joined by his wife who had also woken up. 'Yes yes, please get rid of him,' she begged. 'We'll be ever so grateful to you!'

'I'll do my best,' said Kulfi Ram. 'But you must help me too. You must keep out of the way. If the ghost takes a liking to one of you, he'll never leave this place.'

Dhania's mother-in-law shivered. 'Yes yes, we'll both keep out of the way. Promise.'

'And I must have the key to the store so I can catch hold of the ghost and pull him out or he'll remain here for a hundred years.'

Dhania's mother-in-law quickly handed over the key and the two of them hurried back to their room. Kulfi Ram opened the store and told Dhania to come out. Dripping with honey, all sticky and feeling very very cross, Dhania came out and charged into another room thinking it was his. But, oh horrors! it was not his. The room was full of cotton wool all fluffed up to make quilts for the family. The honey acted like gum. Dhania was soon covered with cotton and really began to look like a ghost. From a chink in their door his in-laws were watching. When they saw Dhania covered with cotton, they clutched at each other for sheer fright, ducked their heads and stayed there.

The coast was clear. Kulfi Ram took Dhania to the well behind the house. Dhania had a bath and buried his sticky clothes in a field nearby. Next morning when he got up from bed he looked completely innocent and oh, so clean! Once again he ate little for the morning meal. But on the way back, at the far end of the village, he and Kulfi Ram had a good feed of milk and jalebis. And the two friends went back home, laughing all the way.

A Sweet for Khan

Before 1947, when India and Pakistan were one country, our neighbour on the north-western frontier was Afghanistan. At that time there used to be a flourishing trade between India and Afghanistan. One major item of trade coming in was fruit, mainly the dry variety. Natives of Afghanistan, known as Pathans, came to India with stocks of dry fruit. They lived and traded here during the winter months when their own country was covered with snow. Winter over, they went back with things which would sell in Afghanistan, like cloth and spices. Since Delhi was an important business centre, many Pathans came to Delhi to trade. They were generally warm-hearted people but quick to anger and very careful with money. Here is a story about one such Afghan trader.

*

In the city of Kabul in Afghanistan, there once lived a Pathan. His name was Khan Hyder Khan. But like many other men from Afghanistan, he was commonly addressed as simply Khan.

Khan owned a small shop in a bazaar in Kabul. In that shop he sold dry fruit like almonds, raisins, apricots and figs. Right through summer, Khan sold dry fruit. But just before winter, he closed shop. Packing a good stock of dry fruit, he travelled all the way to India. For the next few months his home was Delhi. In Delhi Khan moved from street to street selling his wares. He was very careful with his money, and drove a hard bargain. And nobody had ever known Khan to let a single paisa go waste.

Now Khan was more than six feet tall. He always wore a turban, with a golden skull cap resting on top of his head. And this added to his height. Clad in a loose salwar kurta and waistcoat, with a flowing beard and moustache, Khan looked fearsome.

People were a little scared of him, specially small children. But Khan did manage to make a few friends. One such friend was a lala (trader) who owned a shop selling cloth. Every time Khan went past the shop, the lala called him in for a chat. They often had tea and samosas together and enjoyed one another's company.

One day the lala got a special sweet for the Khan. It was pale brown in colour and shaped like a ball cut into half. It was so hard that one could not dig a finger into it. But the lala broke off a piece and offered it to Khan. And when Khan put it into his mouth—oh! he was simply delighted. Never before had he tasted anything quite so delicious! He burst into loud praise. The lala offered him another piece and yet another. Khan kept eating and praising the sweet by turns. At last when he had eaten his fill he asked the lala, 'Tell me my friend, what is the name of this heavenly sweet?'

'We call it sohan halwa,' said the lala.

Khan closed his eyes in ecstasy. 'Wah! Sohan halwa! What a name! Sohan halwa. Khan will not forget. *Allah kasam Khan yaad rakhega* (Khan swears by God Almighty he'll remember it)!'

Khan thanked his friend again and again for the sohan halwa. Then, with one last loving look at the remainder of the sweet, he left the shop. But he remembered the sweet. It was simply too delicious to forget. Day and night he thought of it. Sometimes he even dreamt of it. And how he wished to eat it again!

Now Khan knew sohan halwa by colour, shape and size. But he had no idea where to buy it. Nor did he seek his lala friend's advice. He simply made a habit of peeping into shops to see if anyone had sohan halwa for sale.

For days on end Khan looked into shops. He saw a whole lot of things for sale but never sohan halwa. He was beginning to lose heart when one day he saw what he was looking for. Right in front of a small shop, piled in a wooden tray were some twenty pieces of what looked like sohan halwa. True, it was a somewhat dirty looking shop. On one side of the sweet lay a pile of brooms, on the other several coils of rope and a couple of mousetraps. But that did not matter to Khan. He picked up one of the half balls of sohan halwa and dashed into the shop. 'How much for this?' he demanded.

The shopkeeper was busy weighing out rice for another customer but Khan couldn't wait. 'How much for this?' he shouted again. 'Can't you see I'm in a hurry?'

The shopkeeper looked at the half ball in Khan's hand. 'Four annas (twenty-five paise),' he said. Khan dug into his pocket, took out a four-anna bit, handed it to the shopkeeper and dashed out of the shop.

Khan walked fast. With those long legs, this was fast indeed. He walked till he came to an open square at one end of the market.

There was a low wall all around the square. Khan sat down on the wall. With a sigh of sheer happiness he took out the half ball and dug his teeth into it. Almost immediately he spat it out. The sohan halwa was horrible! Khan waited a bit, took another bite and spat it out again. It still tasted horrible.

Khan was thoroughly puzzled. How come this sohan halwa tasted so bad when the one at his lala friend's shop had been pure delight?

Suddenly Khan began to feel very angry about the whole thing. He had spent all of four annas and he was going to make the most of it, come what may. He didn't want to waste money. No sir. So he settled down squarely on the wall and began to munch the halwa, hating every bite but munching with determination all the same.

Just then a man happened to pass by. He was amazed to see the Khan pulling the most awful faces but eating away steadily while bubbles came out of his mouth and nose. 'For heaven's sake, Khan,' cried the man, 'what you are eating is not meant to be eaten. It's soap, man, soap! Why on earth are you eating soap?'

Khan frowned at the interruption. 'You're wrong,' he declared. 'Khan is not eating soap. Khan is eating good money. I spent four annas on the stuff and I'm not going to waste that money.'

The story goes that Khan ate the whole cake of soap. He felt sick for days afterwards. But he had the satisfaction of having made use of his four annas.

Adventure by Midnight

This is a story from rural Bengal. It paints a very realistic picture of the simple village people of Bengal and how they live. Agriculture is their mainstay. They grow their own paddy, and fish and coconuts are much loved delicacies. In Bengal, as in other parts of India, a wedding is a very special event. But day-to-day family life ranks above everything else. And cattle are considered part of the family, since they are such a help to the farmer.

*

In a village in Bengal there lived an old couple known as Kaka Moshai and Kaki Ma. They owned some land and a small house. They also owned two cows and a bullock. The bullock they had named Nitai.

Kaka was tall and walked very straight, in spite of his age. He was a man of few words. Kaki, on the other hand, was short and dumpy and my, but she loved to talk! When she talked too much, Kaka simply went off to work in the fields. Kaka and Kaki had no children but they loved one another. For forty years they had lived together happily in their little thatched house at one end of the village.

But one day Kaka Moshai and Kaki Ma had a terrible fight. It happened like this. Kaka went to the stream near their house for a bath. He had a bath there every morning but on that particular day he had a rare stroke of luck. He floated his gamchha (towel) in the water and a fish swam straight into the folds. Kaka was overjoyed. He loved fish curry. Grabbing the fish with both hands, gamchha and all, he ran back home. Kaki was sweeping the veranda in front of the house. Kaka boomed, 'Never in your life will you get a katla (a kind of fish) as fresh as this! Turn it into one of your special curries, with lots of coconut and green chillies. I'll eat a little early today.'

Kaki put away her broom. She cleaned the fish, ground the spices, scraped the coconut, slit the green chillies, heated the oil and hey presto! the curry was soon bubbling on the fire. A delicious aroma filled the air. It even reached Kaka Moshai as he worked in the fields and filled him with happiness. 'That woman,' he said to himself, 'she sure knows how to cook!'

Kaka was right. Kaki was a wonderful cook. But that day her heart was not in the cooking. She had just received a postcard to say that her brother's son was to be married shortly. Not only that. He was to be married to a girl from Calcutta. Kaki was most excited about it. A girl from Calcutta! So the wedding would be a grand affair. The bride would be wearing the most gorgeous clothes and ornaments. So would the other women. And what should she wear? Her white sari with the broad red border?

Kaki kept thinking of her sari when she should have been thinking of the fish. Meantime the curry boiled away merrily on the fire. Slowly the water dried up and the pieces of fish began to burn. Once again the smell reached Kaka Moshai as he tilled his fields and he came charging back like a bull in a temper. One look at the pan on the fire and he burst out, 'So you've burnt the lovely fish I got this morning! You careless woman! Can't you cook a simple thing like fish curry?'

Kaki answered back, 'So I can't cook a simple thing like fish curry, is it? And may I ask who has been cooking for Your Majesty these forty years?'

'Fine. You've cooked for me all these years. But does that give you a right to burn things now? And my favourite dish at that? Can't you be more careful?'

Kaki shouted, 'I work for you day after day, from dawn to dusk, and this is how you repay me? You ungrateful man! You—!'

They fought and fought till Kaka was out of breath. He simply wasn't used to talking so much. So he turned on his heel and made for the fields again. But Kaki wasn't finished yet. She glared at his back and announced grimly, 'You've insulted me. I shall not speak to you again till Nitai's horns turn blue!'

Kaki went around the kitchen, banging pots and pans till she had cooled down a bit. Then she threw out the charred fish and put some potatoes on to boil for the midday meal.

Kaka did not utter a word as he ate. Neither did Kaki. When Kaka had eaten, he went and lay down under the jackfruit tree behind the house. Kaki cleaned the vessels and swept the kitchen. Then she lay down in the courtyard, with her feet in the sun. And tired as she was, Kaki soon fell asleep.

When Kaki woke up, the sun had just gone behind the tops of the coconut trees. It was late afternoon. Time for tea. She opened her mouth to call out to Kaka. But suddenly she remembered her words, 'I shall not speak to you till Nitai's horns turn blue.' She could not go back on her words. Kaki realized that she had made a terrible mistake. Here she was, dying to talk to Kaka, but how was it possible after what she had told him? Fat chance there was of Nitai's horns turning blue! Whoever heard of a thing like that? The horns would remain as grey as ever.

One more day went by without Kaka and Kaki saying a word to one another. And then Kaki knew she could not stand the silence any longer. She was so used to chatting with Kaka, telling him little things that happened around the house, asking for his opinion, waiting for a word of praise when she cooked something for him. She simply could not bear the thought of not being on speaking terms with Kaka. Kaki made up her mind. Since Nitai's horns would not turn blue on their own, she would have to colour them. She had a small bag of washerman's blue which she used on Kaka's white clothes. Now she decided to use this on Nitai's horns.

Kaki could not dream of doing the job in the daytime. Kaka made several trips to the cowshed every day, to make sure all was well with his precious cattle. If he saw Kaki painting Nitai's horns, he would never stop making fun of her. No, the job would have to be done at night.

Kaki waited till the night was far gone. In the other bed Kaka was fast asleep. He was even snoring. 'Now's my chance,' thought Kaki. She rolled out of the bed, tiptoed to the back door, opened it ever so softly and stepped out into the dark. It was like stepping into a well. Kaki could hardly see where she was going. There was no moon and the sky was covered with clouds, so even the stars were blocked out. A wind had sprung up. It shook the trees and made them look like ghosts. Kaki was terrified. But she said her prayers, wrapped her sari tight around herself and kept going. She had something important to do and that gave her courage.

The cowshed stood behind the house. Kaki reached it and opened the door. She took out the bag of blue and emptied the contents into an earthen platter. Feeling her way about, she cupped her hands and took a little water from a pail that stood in one corner. Making a paste of blue and water, Kaki spread it thickly on Nitai's horns.

Completely satisfied with herself, Kaki turned to go. But as she neared the door she suddenly saw a human form blocking the way. Kaki threw up her hands and screamed and screamed till Nitai and the two cows joined in the uproar. And there was such a racket in the cowshed that it almost drowned Kaka's voice. 'Stop that noise!' he boomed. 'At once!'

At the very sound of Kaka's voice Kaki was her old self again. 'Oh, so it's you?' she said. 'And what are you doing here, in the cowshed, at the dead of night?'

'Looking for a bag of blue,' said Kaka. 'Didn't you say you wouldn't speak to me till Nitai's horn turned blue?' And Kaka burst out laughing. Kaki began to laugh too. Leaving Nitai and the cows to figure out what had happened, Kaka and Kaki walked back to the house. And both were chatting as hard as they could.

The Unwanted Guest

Here is a folk-tale from Andhra Pradesh. It was originally told in Telugu, the language of the people of Andhra. It highlights the fact that a village priest is generally a poor man and finds it difficult to support his family. But it also points out that even in olden times women could solve their own problems. They stayed at home and rarely ventured out. But when necessary, they could outwit men. There are similar folk-tales in other Indian languages where women are shown to be very intelligent and resourceful.

*

This is a story of a woman called Buddhimati. She lived in a village in Andhra Pradesh. The word Buddhimati means 'a woman of intelligence' and Buddhimati really was as good as her name. At any rate, she was far, far more intelligent than her husband Vishnu Rao.

Vishnu Rao was a brahmin. He worked as a priest. And, like so many other village priests, he earned just enough to provide his family with one square meal a day. Sometimes he failed to earn even that much. But in spite of his poverty, he loved to invite people to his house for meals. Friend, acquaintance, neighbour, neighbour's cousin, anybody. Vishnu Rao only had to meet someone in the street to bring him home for a meal. Many people took advantage of his hospitality. They pretended to be hungry or down and out so as to get a free meal.

Now there was precious little food in Vishnu Rao's house at the best of times. With this steady stream of guests pouring in, Buddhimati often had to go hungry herself. Sometimes even her children had to go hungry so the guest could eat. Buddhimati did not like this at all. She begged and pleaded with Vishnu Rao to change his ways. But her begging and pleading had no effect. Day after day he continued to bring unwanted guests. And night after night Buddhimati lay awake trying to think of a way out of the problem.

At last Buddhimati had an idea. And so excited was she about it that once again she lay awake all night. She even began to wait

eagerly for the next uninvited guest. She didn't have long to wait. The following afternoon, when Vishnu Rao came home from work, there was another brahmin tagging along after him. 'We want lunch,' said Vishnu Rao as he entered. 'We are both very hungry.'

Buddhimati smiled broadly, 'But of course. Who wouldn't be hungry after working hard in the morning? Lunch is ready. As soon as you've had a bath, you can eat.'

Vishnu Rao was puzzled. He looked at his wife and thought to himself, 'I've brought an uninvited guest and yet this woman has not grumbled or pulled a face. What's the matter?' All the same he was happy to see her in such a cheerful mood. Vishnu Rao spread out a mat for his guest. 'Please be seated,' he said. 'I'll be back in no time.' And off he went to the river for a bath.

The guest settled down on the mat. For a while he heard pots and pans being banged around in the kitchen. Then Buddhimati came into the room. She swept one corner of the room and smeared it with cowdung paste. Next she brought a stout wooden stick, the kind used for washing clothes, and stood it in the corner. She lighted an earthen lamp before the stick and made offerings of rice, plantains and flowers. Folding her hands, she bowed low before the stick and seemed to be saying a prayer.

The brahmin had never before seen anything like this. He honestly thought Buddhimati had gone out of her mind. 'What on earth are you trying to do?' he asked. Buddhimati simply waved one hand, asking him to be quiet. She continued to perform her pooja before the stick. Finally she turned to the brahmin and said, 'Forgive me for behaving like this. But I always worship the stick in this manner when my husband brings home a guest.'

'Why?' asked the brahmin, his heart beating a little faster.

By way of an answer Buddhimati said simply, 'If I purify the stick with a pooja, then the gods will forgive my husband for beating up the guest.'

The brahmin jumped up in alarm. 'Beating up the guest?' he cried, almost choking over his words. 'Do you mean to tell me that your husband does this as a habit?'

'You must forgive him, sir,' begged Buddhimati with folded hands. 'He's slightly mad. But only slightly. He doesn't mean to hurt his guests. He loves them dearly . . . Why sir, what's happened?'

But the guest had already shot out of the door, carrying his chappals in one hand because he didn't want to waste time putting them on. Vishnu Rao was just coming back from the river. He was amazed to see the brahmin running away. 'What's happened?' he asked his wife. 'That man was supposed to have his lunch here.'

'I think he got annoyed. He wanted the stick but I refused to give it to him. Without that stick how will I wash the family's dirty clothes?'

Vishnu Rao struck his forehead with one hand. 'O you foolish woman, you've insulted my guest. And a guest is like a god. When will you ever learn? Here, give me that stick. I'll run after him and present it to him personally.'

Vishnu Rao grabbed the stick and began to run after the brahmin. 'Wait, wait,' he called out, 'don't disappoint me. I say, wait!'

The brahmin looked over his shoulder. Seeing Vishnu Rao running after him, armed with a stick, he ran faster than ever. In a few minutes he had disappeared from view. Vishnu Rao came back a dejected man. He scolded Buddhimati some more for refusing to give the guest what he had asked for. Then he had his meal and forgot all about the incident.

But the brahmin did not forget. He went around whispering in people's ears, 'Never, never go to Vishnu Rao's house for a meal. The fellow will first feed you and then hammer you with a stick, good and hard.' People believed him. They stopped accepting Vishnu Rao's invitations. And that is how Buddhimati finally got rid of unwanted guests.

Why Pigs Are So Dirty

Meghalaya is one of the easternmost states of India. It is heavily forested and rich in natural beauty and wildlife. The people of Meghalaya have a treasure trove of folk-tales about animals. In these tales they often find an amusing explanation for some natural phenomenon. We are all familiar with the expression 'dirty pig'. The following story from Meghalaya tells us the reason why pigs are so dirty.

*

The north-eastern region of India is one long stretch of forest land. Lying at the foot of the Himalayas, it receives plenty of rain. So the trees and bushes grow lush and green. Once upon a time, in this forest there lived a whole lot of animals—tigers, leopards, rhinos, deer, rabbit, wild buffalo and wild pig. The tiger was the king and all the other animals lived in fear of him.

But to tell you the truth, the tiger was rather a good king. He did not kill except to satisfy his hunger. When his stomach was full he used to walk lazily through the forest, humming a tune. He even smiled at the other animals as they went about their business.

One day the tiger killed a wild buffalo. And he ate till he was ready to burst. When the meal was over, he went to a forest pool to drink some water. As chance would have it, a plump and frisky young pig had also gone to the same pool to drink water. The pig caught a glimpse of the tiger and it gave him the jitters. He held his breath and stood perfectly still, hoping that the tiger would not see him.

But the tiger had already seen him. How could he miss such a plump young pig, frisking among the bushes? The tiger licked his lips. 'Ah,' he said, 'now that's a meal fit for the king of the forest! It shouldn't be difficult to catch him, either. One leap across the pool and that will be the end of young Master Pig. Or is it Miss Pig? Well well, we'll know soon enough. . . But I mustn't frighten him or he'll never come to this pool again.' With this in mind, the tiger slowly walked away, pretending he had not seen the pig at all.

When the last little bit of the tiger's tail had disappeared among the bushes, the pig began to breathe freely again. His courage also flowed back. And with his courage came a flash of piggy pride. He cocked his head to one side and said aloud, 'Now why do you think the tiger went away like that? Not because he didn't see me. No sir! It was because the very sight of me sent him on the run. He's grown old and weak. What is he as compared to a strapping young pig like me?' And the pig flexed his muscles. 'Come to think of it, the tiger should now resign from the post of king,' the pig went on. 'He should give a chance to an up and coming pig like me! It is I who should be king of the forest, with all those animals working as my servants!'

At the very thought of having so many servants, the pig strutted to the edge of the pool and called out, 'You there! Call yourself a tiger, do you? Why are you running away then? Come and fight, you coward, or else hand over your kingdom to me. . . .'

Luckily the tiger's tummy was full and he was in good mood. So he did not come charging after the pig. He only grunted and said over his shoulder, 'Young fellow, if it's a fight you want, I'm more than willing. Come back in two days for the fight of your life. Same time, same place.'

'Done!' squealed the pig, more puffed up than ever. 'You have two more days to live, Mr Tiger. Make the most of it!' And feeling mighty pleased with himself, the pig bounded back to his friends in the forest.

They were all surprised to see him so happy. 'What on earth's happened?' they asked. 'Have you been feeding on green bamboo shoots or bananas or something? You seem to be on top of the world.'

The pig twirled his tail. 'You'd better treat me with more respect,' he said. 'I am the future king of the forest.'

'The WHAT?' laughed his friends.

'The future king of the forest. Do you know what happened today? I met the old tiger by the pool. I challenged him to a fight but he got scared and ran away. We've agreed to fight it out in two days' time. The old fellow's as good as gone. I'll kill him with a single swipe and then I shall be king. . . Why, what's wrong?'

All his friends were staring at him with eyes as big as saucers. One of them managed to say between chattering teeth, 'W-w-what? You actually challenged the tiger to a fight? Are you crazy?'

Others joined in. 'Yes yes, the tiger must've let you off because he wasn't hungry. But next time he'll catch you by the neck and gobble you up. See if he doesn't.'

When all his friends said the same thing, the pig realized that they could be right. He began to shake with fright. 'Oh my goodness!' he wailed, 'what have I gone and done? I shall run away from this forest. Never, never shall I go back to the pool again!'

'That is something you mustn't do,' returned his friends. 'If the tiger doesn't find you at the pool, he'll declare war on pigs. He'll hunt out and kill each one of us. You asked for trouble by challenging the tiger. Now you had better face the consequences.'

By now the young pig was scared out of his wits. 'Won't you at least suggest a way out?' he begged. 'I know I've been very stupid, but surely you can help me a teeny weeny bit?'

'We'd like to help,' said his friends, 'but we just can't think of a way out. . . Why don't you ask grandfather pig?'

The young pig lost no time. He went running to grandfather pig and told him the whole story. Grandfather pig was in the middle of his lunch. But he took time off to give the young pig a good scolding. 'You nitwit!' he yelled, 'first you act crazy enough to challenge the tiger and then you came running to me for help. How many times have you been told never to go anywhere near a tiger? But you young fellows are all the same. You imagine there's nobody as strong and clever as you. Well, go and fight the tiger now!'

The young pig fell at the feet of his grandfather. 'Please, please do something this time, Grandpa. I'll never act so foolish in future. Promise.'

Grandpa softened a bit. 'Okay, let me think,' he grunted.

He bowed his head and sat thinking for some time. At last he looked up and said, 'Hm. Here's a dodge you can try. If your luck is in, the tiger may let you go.'

The pig danced around his grandfather for sheer joy. 'Oh please, please tell me,' he begged. 'I'll do anything you say.'

Grandfather pig dropped his voice to a whisper. 'Look here. Before you go to the pond to meet the tiger, make yourself as dirty as you can. Let's see what happens then.'

The young pig jumped at the idea. Just before his date with the tiger he rolled in mud and slush, dried himself out and rolled again and yet again. When he finally reached the pool he didn't look like a pig at all. He was one big blob of dirt.

The tiger was already there, waiting for his meal to appear. But when he saw the lump of dirt before him he was taken aback. 'What. . . What. . . Who on earth are you?' he asked. 'I've never seen anything like you before.'

'Your Majesty' came the answer, 'it is I, the young pig who was to meet you here.'

The tiger looked at the pig again and wrinkled his nose in disgust. Gone were his dreams of a delicious meal of pig meat! All he wanted was to get rid of the filthy creature before him 'Off with you!' he roared. 'I don't want to look at you. And don't you dare come near me again.'

The young pig managed to get away, though his legs were shaking with fright. He ran to grandfather pig and thanked him with all his heart. Then all the pigs in the forest held a meeting and passed a resolution that in future they would remain as dirty as possible, so the tiger would not be tempted to eat them.

And that is why, to this day, pigs like to wallow in dirt.

A Trip to Heaven

Here is a story that originally came from Bihar. It has everything to please the heart of a common man—reality, religion, fantasy, luck and laughter. There was great economic pressure on the common 'man in old-time Bihar. Folk-tales such as this one helped to lighten the burden and to provide an escape from the drudgery of daily existence.

*

Chhajju was a poor farmer. He owned a small plot of land on which he grew seasonal vegetables like brinjals, pumpkins and cauliflower. It wasn't much but for Chhajju it was enough. He worked hard and slept well, for he was a contented man at heart.

One particular winter Chhajju grew a super crop of cauliflower. People came from far and near to admire the fresh, creamy looking, snow-white heads of cauliflower. One day Chhajju's wife told him, 'Our crop is the talk of the entire village and of many other villages nearby. I'm afraid someone might try to steal it. Why don't you. sleep in the fields at night?'

Chhajju thought this a jolly good idea. Right in the middle of his fields he raised a platform of bamboo and thatch. On this platform he spread a sheet and his bed was ready. That evening, after the family had eaten, Chhajju left his wife and children in his hut, walked to the platform and climbed up. Tired after the day's work, he soon fell asleep. He slept soundly till the crack of dawn. Then he walked back to his hut to start another day. The same thing happened the following night.

On the third night Chhajju went to sleep on the platform as usual, but in the middle of the night something disturbed him. He sat up. It was quiet all around. The entire village was asleep.

Even the jackals in the forest beyond had fallen silent. What had disturbed him then? Chhajju looked around and suddenly caught his breath in surprise. A shining white cloud was slowly coming down from the sky. As Chhajju watched, the cloud headed straight for his fields and made a perfect landing among the cauliflowers. And out stepped, of all things, an elephant! But it was no ordinary elephant, grey in colour. This one glowed as though made of silver. The elephant stretched out its trunk, uprooted a cauliflower and daintily placed it in its mouth. Then another and yet another. Chhajju watched helplessly as the elephant ate up some twenty heads of cauliflower. Having had its fill, the elephant stepped inside the cloud again. The cloud slowly floated up into the sky and was soon lost to view.

For a long time Chhajju sat in a daze. As soon as he had recovered, he raced home to tell his wife what he had seen. The poor woman was fast asleep. Chhajju shook her awake and told her everything. But she wouldn't believe him. 'You must have been dreaming. Whoever heard of a silver elephant stepping out of a shining white cloud? And eating cauliflowers? Bah!'

The following night Chhajju lay awake on the platform. Sure enough the elephant came again. As before, he ate his fill of cauliflower and went back the way he had come. Chhajju raced back home to tell his wife, 'The elephant came again,' he cried. 'I couldn't have had the same dream two nights running. I'm telling you, the elephant was real.'

This time his wife believed him. She said, 'I think that elephant came straight from heaven. He belongs to Indra, king of the gods, and his name is Aeravat.' Chhajju was listening dumbfounded. His wife was the daughter of a pundit and knew a lot about such things. Suddenly she clutched his arm. 'Listen,' she whispered excitedly, 'the elephant comes from heaven and goes back to heaven. Of that I'm certain. Next time it comes, why don't you hang on to its tail and take a trip to heaven? You can come back the following night. I can't go because of the children but *you* mustn't lose this opportunity.'

A little more persuasion from his wife and Chhajju agreed. He was scared stiff at the thought of flying up into the sky at the end of an elephant's tail. But somehow he picked up the courage to do so. The following night, when the elephant entered the cloud to go back to heaven, there was Chhajju hanging on to its tail.

Chhajju spent a full twenty-four hours in heaven and what a glorious time he had! Heaven was a beautiful place. The streets were paved with silver, the palaces were made of gold. When he got tired walking, he had only to wash at one of the many clear, cool streams to feel refreshed again. The air was full of birdsong and the scent of flowers. But what Chhajju enjoyed most of all was his visit to the kitchen. Right in the middle of the kitchen of heaven stood a giant dish of halwa Oh, that halwa was unbeatable! Piping hot and sweet and flavoured with cardamom. And you could eat to bursting because there was so much of it and nobody to stop you. So Chhajju ate and he ate and he ate . . . .

When Chhajju came back to earth via the elephant's tail he walked as in a dream. It was not only the things that he had seen, it was the halwa that he had eaten. He could not think of anything else. That night he hardly slept. Day dawned. Instead of going to work in his fields, Chhajju went and sat in front of his hut. Some of the other men from the village passed by on their way to work. 'How come you're sitting around?' they asked. Chhajju yawned. 'Can't move,' he said lazily. 'Had too much halwa yesterday. Oh, it was great!'

The men were amazed. 'Too much halwa? You had too much halwa, you said? Where on earth was this?'

Some more men had joined them. They all gathered around Chhajju and asked, 'Where did you find all that halwa? Tell us. Surely you can't eat it all by yourself?'

Now Chhajju's wife had warned-him not to talk about the halwa to anyone. But with so many people asking him for details, he forgot all about the warning. 'I had halwa in heaven,' he said proudly.

The other farmers thought Chhajju had gone out of his mind. 'Halwa in heaven?' they repeated. 'This is nothing but a disorder of the brain. You had better go to the vaid ji(doctor) and get yourself treated.'

'Disorder of the brain? Vaid ji?' cried Chhajju. 'What do you mean? I'm telling the truth.'

Bit by bit the farmers were convinced that Chhajju was indeed telling the truth. One by one they dropped their hoes and sat down in a tight circle around Chhajju. 'Look Chhajju,' they said, 'you are a great man. The elephant of Lord Indra himself came to feed in your fields. And you actually enjoyed a trip to heaven. But we are your friends and you must share your good fortune with us. All of us want to go to heaven with you.' And there was a real uproar as all the men joined in and yelled, 'Yes yes, Chhajju, we want to go to heaven with you!'

Chhajju had never received so much attention in his life. He got all puffed up. Without a moment's thought he said, 'Sure, sure. Why not? When the elephant comes at night you can all go with me to heaven. I'll catch the elephant's tail. The next man catches my kurta, the next one catches his kurta and so on. We'll form a line and fly to heaven to eat our fill of halwa.'

There was a wild shout from the men gathered around him. Naturally, the news spread like fire. All the men of the village had a nice long bath at the river and got into their best clothes. The women were not going, neither were the children. But they all wanted a share in the halwa. The men offered to bring some in their pockets. But how much can a pocket hold? And they couldn't carry bags for both their hands had to be free to hang on to the kurta of the man in front. Here was a problem indeed till someone

thought of a sling bag. The women spent the entire day making sling bags out of sacking, old saris, old pajamas. When evening came, the men stood in a line near Chhajju's fields, hearts thumping, mouths dry with excitement.

The night wore on. It became very dark. At first jackals howled in the forest beyond the village. But in time they fell silent. Even the village dogs stopped barking. Everything was quiet when a gasp went up from all the men. The shining white cloud was coming down slowly, ever so slowly. It made a perfect landing among the cauliflowers and out stepped a silver elephant . . . .

The men waited patiently and in total silence till the elephant had eaten its fill. Then Chhajju ran forward and caught the elephant's tail. There was a bit of a scramble as every man tried to catch hold of Chhajju's kurta. But soon they fell in line. Each had a firm grip on the kurta of the man before him. Slowly the cloud rose in the air. With it rose the elephant and Chhajju and, one by one, all the men, down to the last one who was the fat man of the village. Hey presto, they were airborne! And my, but were they wild with excitement!

The journey to heaven was long and the men had waited all day for the promised halwa. So halfway up to heaven their patience gave out. The fat man in particular was feeling very anxious. Would there be any halwa left for him or would those in front finish it all before he got a chance? He asked the man directly in front, 'Are you sure there will be enough halwa for all of us?'

'How do I know?' came the reply.

'Ask the fellow in front.'

'How do I know?' said the fellow in front.

'Ask the fellow in front.'

And so the question went from man to man, right up the line till it reached the man directly behind Chhajju. He asked Chhajju, 'Will there be enough halwa for all of us?'

'Oh plenty,' said Chhajju. 'More than enough for all of us.'

The news travelled back to the fat man. For a while he was quiet. Then he couldn't stand it any longer. 'Why can't Chhajju be more clear about it?' he grumbled. 'Why doesn't he tell us exactly how much halwa there was?'

Once again the question travelled up the line till it reached Chhajju. '*Arre baba,*' said Chhajju, slightly irritated, 'haven't I told you there was lots of halwa?'

The news travelled back and for a while the fat man was quiet. But not for long. The journey did not seem to end and he was tired and hungry. So he jerked at the kurta of the man in front. 'Ask Chhajju one last question. Just how much halwa can I eat in heaven?'

The question travelled up the line once again. But by the time it reached Chhajju, he had lost his patience. He threw out his arms as far as they could go and yelled, 'So much halwa!' The elephant's tail shot out of his grasp and all the men came tumbling down to earth. The fat man came first and all the others landed on top of him. There was a series of loud thuds and then all was quiet. For a while they all lay there, stunned. Then slowly they picked themselves up, dusted their clothes and went back home, grumbling at the fat man for asking silly questions. That was the end of their dream of eating halwa, for sad to say, the elephant never came again.

The Pandavas in the Forest

The following legend comes from the Mahabharat, the Indian epic that is world-famous. The Mahabharat is the saga of the Kuru dynasty. It tells the story of the lifelong enmity between the offshoots of the dynasty—the Pandavas and the Kauravas, who stood for the forces of good and evil respectively. Duryodhan, the crafty Kaurava prince, invited his cousin, the Pandava Yudhishtir, to a game of dice, and using foul means, defeated him. As a forfeit, the Pandavas were banished to the forest for twelve long years. This legend recounts one of the experiences of the noble and righteous Pandavas during their years of exile.

*

With a heavy heart, Yudhishtir donned the garb of an ascetic and left for the forest. He was accompanied by his wife Draupadi and four younger brothers, Bhim, Arjun, Nakul and Sahdev. With the princes went their priest Dhaumya, as did a number of brahmins and a whole crowd of people who loved the Pandavas dearly and hated to see them go.

But Yudhishtir was not happy to see so many people leave hearth and home for his sake. When they reached the edge of the forest, he turned to them and said with folded hands, 'We are deeply grateful to you for all the affection that you have showered on us. But my brothers and I feel that we don't deserve it. We are but ordinary mortals. It is your regard for us that makes us seem like great men, to be followed wherever we go. I beg of you, please return to your families. They need you and you must look after them. You must also look after the elders of our family.

They need you too. If you don't go back and take care of them, who will?'

Some more persuasion and Yudhishtir's subjects reluctantly agreed to return to their homes. His attendants also went back. But the brahmins remained with the Pandavas. Much as Yudhishtir coaxed them to return, they would not agree. They had vowed to serve the Pandavas during the years of banishment, On that first night of exile at the edge of the forest, the brahmins lighted a fire, sang hymns in praise of God and comforted the Pandavas in their grief.

The following morning, as the Pandavas were about to enter the forest, Yudhishtir turned to the brahmins again and said with great humility, 'We have lost all our wealth. For the next twelve years we must live in the forest, with nothing to eat save wild roots and fruit. How can I feed you? And it would break my heart not to be able to provide for you. I can't even ask my brothers to gather fruits for you, for they are suffering so much as it is.'

But the brahmins refused to go back. 'We wish to serve you and keep you company in these years of trial,' they said. 'Even God does not turn away his devotees. Don't you send us back, O king. And don't you worry about food for us, either. We shall fend for ourselves.' After that Yudhishtir could not possibly turn them away. But he felt that the brahmins were his guests and it was his duty to feed them. The problem was, where could he get such a large quantity of food, right in the middle of the forest?

Nevertheless they pressed on, walking over thorns, braving the chill of night and heat of day, and making light of the presence of wild animals. The Pandavas themselves never had enough to eat. They were princes by birth, used to the choicest food and not to pangs of hunger. Being highly disciplined men they never complained, but their faces slowly lost their glow. The brave Arjun began to lose his warlike bearing and Yudhishtir his royal presence.

Even Bhim, that giant among men, who seemed capable of facing any hardship, now began to look tired and spent.

Draupadi saw all this and her anguish deepened by the day. Being a woman, she felt it her duty to feed the men. But what could she do, with not a grain of rice or wheat to be had and nothing but roots, leaves and fruit to offer at every meal?

Draupadi's anguish soon began to show in her face. One day as she sat in the forest, feeling very dejected indeed, the bushes before her parted and out stepped Narad Muni, messenger of the gods, Draupadi ran forward to touch his feet. One look at her and Narad Muni knew something was wrong. 'What is it, my daughter?' he asked. Fighting back her tears (for she was a very courageous woman) Draupadi related her tale of woe. Narad Muni listened attentively. At the end of it he told her, 'My child, why don't you pray to the sun god? He provides food for all the creatures who walk the earth. He will help you.'

From the very next day Draupadi started her worship of the sun god. She had a bath at the crack of dawn. Then, without taking so much as a sip of water, she went and stood waist-deep in the river Ganga. Facing east, she sang hymns in praise of the sun god. As the sun rose, Draupadi made offerings of freshly gathered flowers and fruit. 'O lord,' she murmured with bowed head, 'you are the very life of the universe. I beg of you to answer my prayers. I beseech you, O lord, bestow on me food enough to feed my family and the brahmins who are our guests.'

For days on end Draupadi prayed with deep devotion. And then one morning the sun god himself came to her, walking over the golden waters of the Ganga. Draupadi bowed very low before the dazzling presence. Hands raised in blessing, the sun god told her, 'Go my daughter, your wish shall be granted. I shall provide you with food right through these twelve years.' With these words he gave her a vessel of burnished copper. 'Take this akshay paatra (vessel of plenty),' he said. 'It will fill up with good food for every meal and will remain full till everyone has eaten. But once the vessel is washed and put away, it will not yield any more food till the next meal.'

With these words the sun god disappeared. But Draupadi had got what she wanted most of all and her happiness knew no bounds. The copper vessel filled up at every meal. The brahmins were served first because they were guests of the family. The Pandava princes ate next. As was the custom of the times, the woman of the house, Draupadi, ate last of all, after she had served everyone else. When she was done and the vessel was washed clean, there was no more food till the next meal.

With enough to eat, the men were at peace. So was Draupadi. The sun god had blessed them with food, and they counted themselves very fortunate indeed.

For some time everything went well but Duryodhan was still busy plotting against the Pandavas. He simply did not want them to live in peace. To find out how they were faring in exile, he sent his spies to the forest. In due course the spies came back. 'Maharaj,' they told Duryodhan, 'the Pandavas have made an ashram (hermitage) for themselves and are as well as can be imagined. Twice a day they eat their fill of good, nourishing food. Not only they, but also a whole lot of brahmins who are their guests. The Pandavas and Draupadi are in the pink of health and seem to be perfectly happy and content.'

'How is that possible?' demanded Duryodhan roughly, 'Didn't you find out?'

'We did, Maharaj,' said the chief spy. And the story of the akshay paatra came tumbling out. Duryodhan was consumed with jealousy. He could not bear to think of the Pandavas living in comfort and enjoying good food even in the heart of the forest. And he began to think of ways and means of doing them further harm.

The following day there came to the palace of Duryodhan the sage Durvasa, who was universally dreaded for his foul temper. When angry, Durvasa pronounced terrible curses on whoever had angered him and those curses always came true. In other words, to annoy sage Durvasa in any way meant certain disaster.

Duryodhan gave Durvasa a royal welcome, bending very low to touch the sage's feet and begging him to stay at the palace for as long as he could. Pleased with the courtesy extended to him, Durvasa agreed. He and his numerous disciples were lodged in luxury within the palace and Duryodhan himself attended on the sage to make sure he did not want for anything.

Durvasa was a very difficult guest. All at once he would say, 'I'm hungry. Bring me food this minute.' But when the food was placed before him, he would push it away saying he didn't want it. On coming from his early morning bath he would demand a sumptuous meal for all his disciples and fly into a rage if there was a moment's delay. Few people could tolerate the whims of

Durvasa but Duryodhan put up with everything. At the end of it all Durvasa was so pleased that he said, 'Duryodhan, ask of me any boon that you desire and you shall have it.'

This was just what Duryodhan had hoped for. Touching the sage's feet he said, 'Maharaj, Yudhishtir is my cousin. He is older than me and a very righteous man. But he lives far away in the forest, with his wife and brothers. I beg of you, honour him by being his guest, just as you have honoured me.'

Durvasa agreed readily. Duryodhan went on, 'Maharaj, I beg that you go to the Pandavas's ashram after the brothers, their brahmin guests and Draupadi have all eaten their morning meal. That way you will find them relaxed and free to serve you.' Durvasa said he would remember to do just that. He took his leave and left the palace. Duryodhan was delighted to think that the Pandavas would not be able to offer a meal to Durvasa and would therefore be roundly cursed by him.

Accompanied by no less than ten thousand followers, Durvasa arrived at the forest home of the Pandavas. The Pandava brothers, the brahmins and Draupadi had all finished their morning meal and the akshay paatra had been washed and put away till the evening. Yudhishtir saw the sage from a distance and ran to touch his feet. Durvasa raised one hand in blessing and curtly informed Yudhishtir, 'My disciples and I are going to the river for a bath. Make sure you have a meal ready and waiting for us when we come back.'

Yudhishtir sought out Draupadi. 'Sage Durvasa is here with his ten thousand followers. He wants food for everyone on his return from the river after a bath. Can anything be done about it?' he asked anxiously.

Draupadi froze. She knew that the sage had every right to expect hospitality from her. But how could she possibly feed him and his army of followers after the akshay paatra had been washed and put away? Draupadi was in a tight corner and there seemed to be no way out. The more she thought about it, the worse she felt. If the sage got annoyed, he might pronounce a curse and reduce them all to ashes!

In her despair, Draupadi's thoughts turned to Krishna, lord of the universe. Krishna had taken human form and was the king of Dwarka. He always came to Draupadi's aid when she was in trouble and prayed to him. Now Draupadi folded her hands and prayed, 'O Krishna, you are my only refuge. You and you alone can protect me and my family from the sage's anger. Help me out, I beseech you!'

Draupadi's prayer reached Krishna in faraway Dwarka and he immediately appeared before her in her forest home. Draupadi was beside herself with joy to see Krishna. She began to tell him how she simply could not provide a meal for Durvasa and his disciples. But Krishna cut her short. 'Draupadi,' he said, 'I have no time for your stories just now. Give me something to eat this minute. I'm also terribly hungry!'

Draupadi was most embarrassed. Here was Lord Krishna himself, asking for something to eat and she had nothing to offer. Shame-faced, she said, 'My lord, we have all finished our meal. The akshay paatra has been cleaned and put away. It will not yield any more food till the evening. What shall I do?'

'Bring the vessel here,' ordered Krishna. 'I wish to see it for myself.' Draupadi obeyed. Krishna examined the vessel carefully and saw a tiny piece from a single grain of rice still stuck to the edge. Picking it up between finger and thumb, he put the piece in his mouth and swallowed it. 'May this your offering to me, be enough to satisfy the hunger of the entire universe,' he blessed Draupadi. Then, turning to Sahdev who had just come in, Krishna commanded, 'Go to the river and bring sage Durvasa and all his disciples here for a meal.' With these words Krishna disappeared.

Sahdev did as he was told. Meanwhile, Krishna's blessing had borne fruit and suddenly the hunger of every creature on earth was completely satisfied. When Durvasa and his disciples went to the river for a bath, they were very hungry. But when they came out they were totally satiated, as after a full meal. The disciples turned to Durvasa saying, 'Gurudev (great teacher), we are quite full. We can't possibly eat another mouthful!'

For once Durvasa forgot to be angry. 'It's very strange,' he replied, 'but I'm also quite full. I can't eat any more either. But how shall we face Yudhishtir now? He must have arranged for a meal for all of us and it would be a great offence not to partake of it. Yudhishtir is a good man and an ardent devotee of God. If he's angered and curses us, we are done for. I suggest we don't go back to the ashram at all. Let's run away from this place. . . .'

So Durvasa and his disciples took to their heels. Running in the opposite direction, they were soon lost among the trees of the forest. When Sahdev came to the river, there was not a soul around. He went back and informed Draupadi and she smiled for sheer relief, offering a heartfelt prayer of thanks to Krishna who had come to her rescue.

Vishwamitra

In ancient times, India produced many great rishis. Rishis were men who gave up the world and went to live in the forests. They ate very simple food, wore very plain clothes and spent all their time in prayer and meditation. They were men of great learning and spiritual power. A rishi's blessing could bring great fortune and his curse could reduce a man to ashes.

Vashisht and Vishwamitra were two such rishis. Their names are mentioned over and over again in our ancient books—the Ramayan, Mahabharat and the Puranas. The following story tells us how Vishwamitra became a rishi.

*

In ancient times, there lived a mighty king named Vishwamitra. He ruled over a vast empire. He was fabulously rich and had routed in battle every single king who dared oppose him.

One of Vishwamitra's passions was hunting. Nothing gave him greater joy than a day out in the forest, armed with bow and arrow, stalking birds and animals. Once Vishwamitra went out on a hunt. He was accompanied by a large number of courtiers and attendants. All day they wandered in the forest, pushing their way through thorny bushes and long, snake-like creepers that hung from the trees. By the evening they were worn out and desperately looking for a place to rest and have a refreshing drink of water.

Just as the sun was setting in the west, they came to an ashram. It was no more than a bunch of three or four huts standing in a grove of banyan and pipal trees. The walls were made of mud and the roofs thatched with dried grass. The ashram looked deserted.

There was not a soul to be seen. Vishwamitra was doubtful if such a place would be able to provide even a drink of water, let alone something to eat. Perhaps the rishi who lived there or one of his disciples could show them the way to the nearest pond or river.

Vishwamitra had barely reached the first hut when he met Vashisht, one of the greatest sages and teachers of all time. The ashram belonged to him. He welcomed Vishwamitra. 'What brings you here, O king?' he asked. Vishwamitra told him, 'My companions and I are terribly thirsty. Can you help us find water?'

Sage Vashisht replied, 'Yes yes, of course. But why only water? You must be hungry too. Do rest a little and I'll see what I can bring you.'

In a short while the sage was back with a pitcher full of milk. It was so fresh that the foam still bubbled on the surface. And there was more than enough to quench the thirst of King Vishwamitra and all his companions. But Vishwamitra was wondering, 'From where could the rishi have obtained all this fresh, sweet milk? And in such a short while too? There is no habitation nearby. I can't see even a soul in the ashram who could ran errands for the rishi. This is very strange!'

The king's men were equally surprised. They were still talking about it when the rishi came again. 'Your evening meal is served,' he said. 'Please come and eat. You must be very hungry.'

Vishwamitra and his men were led inside another hut, Mats had been laid out against the wall. And before each mat lay a leaf plate piled with the choicest delicacies. Indeed, King Vishwamitra himself had never before tasted food that was quite so delicious. 'This gets more and more mysterious,' thought Vishwamitra to himself. 'Where did all this food come from? There's more than we can ever eat and each dish tastes better than the other!' Once again he noticed his men whispering among themselves and he knew that they were equally mystified. How did the rishi manage to produce so much food for them without any help at all, and in next to no time?

By the time they finished their meal, night had fallen. It was too dark to find their way home. Besides, a whole day of walking, followed by a sumptuous meal, had made them all very drowsy. They were getting ready to lie down on the earthen floor when Sage Vashisht informed them, 'Please retire to the next hut. You will find the beds much softer and more comfortable than the hard floor.'

Morning found Vishwamitra and his men rested after a good night's sleep. And all the questions that had been bothering them the previous day came to the surface again. 'Rishivar,' said the king, 'this is more than I can understand. You live in an ashram and your life is simplicity itself. You have no attendants either. How do you manage to look after your guests so well?'

Sage Vashisht smiled and led the king to the eastern side of the ashram. There, on a patch of soft green grass, a cow stood grazing. In the light of the rising sun she seemed to be made of beaten gold. Vishwamitra had never seen a more beautiful or graceful animal. 'She is my Sabala,' said Vashisht. 'The giver of plenty. She gives me whatever I seek, provided I don't seek it for myself.'

Vishwamitra was dumbfounded. Then, recovering himself quickly he said, 'Rishivar, this is very strange. You are an ascetic. Your needs are simple. What for do you keep a cow that provides such luxuries? She is better suited to the palace of a king. I suggest you give the cow to me.'

Vashisht was a man renowned for his patience. He was not offended by Vishwamitra's demand. He only smiled and said, 'Sabala is not an ordinary cow. Her mother is the divine Surabhi who lives in heaven and makes men's wishes come true. Sabala is like my own daughter. She lives under my protection. How can I possibly part with her?'

'I shall give you a thousand cows in return,' said Vishwamitra.

'A thousand cows?' laughed Vashisht. 'I'm not a cowherd. What on earth shall I do with so many of them?'

'But what use is such a valuable cow to you?' Vishwamitra pressed on. 'On the other hand, if she is with me, so many people can derive benefit from her.' Vashisht shook his head in one final gesture of refusal. 'I'm sorry, O king, but you cannot have this cow.'

Vishwamitra's greatest failing was his temper. Now he flew into a rage. 'I am a king,' he shouted. 'And a king has a right to take away anything he likes from his subjects. Still, I'm asking for the cow and not taking her by force. And I promise you, if you let me have her, I'll give you anything you like in return!'

Vashisht was unmoved. He said, 'I give you the honour that is due to you as my king. But even a king cannot always get what he wants.'

Vishwamitra took this to be a gesture of defiance and he was not one to tolerate defiance. Used to having his own way in everything, he ordered two of his attendants, 'Bring that cow to the palace.'

The attendants tried to do as they were told. But Sabala had other ideas. She wrenched herself free and went and stood near

Vashisht, as much as to ask, 'What have I done? Why am I being sent away?' The sage stroked her back to calm her down. Just then Vishwamitra's attendants made the mistake of untying Sabala's calf and walking off with it. They thought that with the calf in their keeping, Sabala would follow them of her own free will. Sabala followed them all right but not as they had expected. She charged at them like a thunderbolt. Using her horns and hoofs to the greatest advantage, she sent the attendants flying in different directions.

Vishwamitra realized that his men were no match for Sabala. But he was not so easily defeated. 'I'm going away,' he informed Vashisht. 'But rest assured I shall be back before long. And when I come next I shall take the cow with me.'

Vishwamitra never gave an idle threat. The very next day he was back again, this time at the head of a large army. But he was in for a rude shock. An army twice the size of his own awaited him at the ashram.

A fierce battle followed. The soldiers of Vishwamitra were hand-picked men. They had few equals anywhere in the land. But the soldiers of Vashisht fought with a ferocity that had not been witnessed before on the face of the earth. With a strength that was superhuman, they fell upon the army of Vishwamitra. Swords clashed, arrows ripped the air, here and there a mace hit a protective shield and shattered it. It was an unequal fight. Vishwamitra's army did not stand a chance. Well before sunset, his army had been utterly defeated. All his soldiers lay dead on the ground.

Never before had Vishwamitra felt so humiliated. He was beside himself with rage and frustration but he managed, somehow, to control himself. He went to Vashisht and asked him, 'How on earth did you manage to vanquish my army? It was invincible.'

Vashisht replied, 'I did nothing. Sabala managed it all. Didn't I tell you she is divine? It was by a divine decree that she came here, to live in my ashram, and no human being can take her away from me.'

At last light dawned on Vishwamitra. He realized that divine power was greater than brute force. Sage Vashisht was stronger than him. Vashisht had something more than gold and an army at his command. He had divine power. Then and there Vishwamitra made up his mind to acquire the same divine power and to become as great a rishi as Vashisht, if not greater. Vishwamitra told Vashisht, 'I admit defeat at your hands, rishivar, and I'm going back where I came from.'

Vashisht raised his hand. 'You will not go alone,' he said. 'Take back all the soldiers who came with you.' And as he said this, every single fallen soldier stood up as from a deep sleep. More impressed than ever and even more determined to develop the same powers as Vashisht, King Vishwamitra went back to his palace.

The following morning Vishwamitra renounced his kingdom and all his wealth. Donning the robes of an ascetic, he went away to the forest. Legend says he prayed and meditated for a thousand years. He practised severe austerities like living on a single meal a month and meditating under a blazing sun, day after day, year after year. He gained great powers, so much so that even the gods began to fear him. But he often fell from grace and lost some of his powers because he flew into a temper. At long last Vishwamitra rose to be like Vashisht, a Brahma rishi, one of the greatest sages who has ever lived.

How Ganga Came Down to Earth

This legend comes from the famous Indian epic Ramayan which tells us the life story of Lord Ram. The Ramayan also tells us the life stories of Ram's ancestors like Bhagirath, who is the hero of this story.

The Ramayan mentions many sages who were men of great learning and spirituality. By practising severe austerities, these sages had acquired almost divine powers. Each of these sages had an ashram of his own, deep within a forest. Kings often sent their sons to stay at an ashram and learn at the feet of a sage.

Vishwamitra was one such sage. Once Ram and his brother Lakshman came to spend some time with Vishwamitra at the latter's ashram. One day, as the three were travelling through the forest, they came to the bank of the sacred river Ganga. The princes requested the sage to relate the story of Ganga. Here is what Vishwamitra told them.

*

Ganga was once a river in heaven. How she was brought from heaven to earth is a wonderful story.

Long ago, there ruled over Ayodhya a king by the name of Sagar. He had two wives. The first wife, Kesini, had one son named Asmanjas. The second wife, Sumati, had as many as sixty thousand sons.

The sons of Sumati grew up to be strong and handsome princes. But they were proud and haughty and nobody liked them. Asmanjas himself turned out to be of unsound mind and very cruel. But his son Anshuman was the exact opposite of his father. He was brave and virtuous and of a very amiable nature.

Meanwhile Sagar was growing more and more powerful. He extended the frontiers of his kingdom far and wide and gathered untold wealth. To establish his supremacy over all the other kings of the region, Sagar performed an aswamedha yagya (horse sacrifice). For the purpose of the yagya, a horse was selected from the royal stable. It really was an animal worthy of a king, tall and immensely strong, with muscles that rippled under its silvery coat.

After days of prayer and a grand havan (ritual fire), a tilak was placed on the forehead of the horse, a garland around its neck and a sweetmeat in its mouth. To the blowing of conches as an auspicious beginning, the horse was released. It was free to wander where it pleased. If any other king or chieftain dared to catch the horse, it meant that he challenged the supremacy of Sagar and a battle would follow. If the horse was allowed to go free, Sagar would be acknowledged the overlord of the entire area that had come under the horse's hoofs. Sagar sent a strong force to follow the horse and give battle to anyone who dared stop it.

No mortal king dared to cross the path of the warlike horse and thus challenge the supremacy of Sagar. But Indra, king of the gods, donned the disguise of a rakshasa(demon) and made off with the animal. Indra was not trying to play a trick. The truth is, the gods regarded a yagya by mortals as a challenge to their superiority. So they tried their best to put obstacles in the way of the yagya so it could not be completed. Moreover, the sixty thousand sons of Sagar had grown into wicked men. It was necessary to rid the world of them. For this dual purpose Indra made a plan, stole the horse and hid it away.

Sagar was greatly upset when he heard that his horse had been stolen. He sent out the sixty thousand sons of Sumati to look for the animal all over the earth. They were told to spare no pains to recover it. 'If the horse is not brought back, the yagya cannot be completed,' said the king gravely. 'What is more, this loss brings great shame and discredit to us. Go and find the horse and bring it back, no matter where it is hidden.'

The sons of Sumati spread out all over the earth and looked and looked. But the horse was nowhere to be found. In their anxiety they even began to dig the earth as for hidden treasure. But of course the horse wasn't there. Utterly dejected, they went back to Sagar and reported their failure. The king was not one to admit defeat. 'Go down and ransack paataal, the nether world,' he ordered.

The princes made their way to the nether world. Soon they came to an ashram. In front of the ashram a sage sat deep in prayer and not far from him, stood the horse, grazing peacefully. The princes had no idea that the man was Kapil Muni, lord of all the sages. They thought they had found not only the horse but also the thief. They rushed at the sage shouting, 'Here's the thief, pretending to be a holy man.' Kapil Muni was rudely disturbed at his prayers. He opened his eyes and glared at the princes. And then and there all sixty thousand of them were reduced to ashes. Indra's dual purpose was thus fulfilled. The wicked princes had been destroyed and due to the absence of the horse, the yagya could not be completed.

King Sagar waited anxiously for the return of the princes who had gone in search of the horse. But he waited in vain. Some time later he called his grandson Anshuman and said, 'Your uncles went to the nether world to look for the horse but they have not returned. I am anxious to know what happened to them. I have great faith in your youth and strength. Go and look for them. Arm yourself well and come back crowned with success!'

The noble Anshuman obeyed his grandfather and set out. Closely following the path taken by the princes, he finally reached the nether world. King Sagar's horse was there all right, grazing contentedly. But why was the place dotted with so many thousands of heaps of ashes? It was a distressing sight.

By and by Anshuman met Garud, king of the birds. Garud informed him, 'Those heaps are all that is left of the sixty thousand sons of Sagar. They were consumed by a single angry glance from Kapil Muni. But take heart. Lead the horse back to your grandfather so that he can complete the yagya.'

'And what about my uncles?' asked Anshuman.

'If you wish the souls of your uncles to enter heaven, their ashes must be washed in the water of the Ganga,' said Garud. 'And for that, my son, the Ganga must be brought down all the way from heaven to the nether world.'

Anshuman rushed home with the horse and told the king all that he had seen and heard. Sagar was plunged into grief to hear of the fate that had befallen his sons. He knew it was nearly impossible to bring Ganga down to paataal and this added to his grief. He somehow managed to complete the yagya but he died a broken man.

After Sagar, Anshuman ascended the throne as king of Ayodhya. He was succeeded by Dilip, and Dilip in turn was succeeded by Bhagirath. Anshuman and Dilip tried their best to bring Ganga down to paataal for the salvation of their forefathers. But their efforts only met with failure and they died grieving over this failure.

Bhagirath was a brave king. He had no children and eagerly desired an heir to continue his line. He had also made up his mind to bring Ganga down to earth, come what may. To that end, he entrusted the kingdom to his ministers and left for the Himalayas to perform penance. And what penance! Bhagirath went through the severest of austerities. He ate only once a month. With a ring of fire burning all around him and his head exposed to the blazing sun, he sat in meditation for days on end.

Brahma was pleased with the penance. He appeared before Bhagirath and asked him, 'What is it that you desire?' Bhagirath fell at the feet of Brahma and said, 'I desire two things. Bless me with a son so the line of my forefathers may not end with me. And please order Ganga to go down to paataal. Cursed by Kapil Muni in paataal, my ancestors were reduced to ashes. Till such time that holy water from the Ganga is poured over these ashes, the souls of my ancestors cannot ascend to heaven. Please, my lord, I await your blessings.'

Brahma replied, 'The gods are pleased with your penance. Both your wishes are granted. But there is one difficulty. Coming from heaven, Ganga must first descend to earth before she goes down to paataal. And the earth cannot withstand the force of her descent. The mighty Shiva alone can stand it. Pray to him.'

Bhagirath renewed his penance and continued for a long time without food or water, praying constantly to Shiva. At last he won Shiva's grace. Appearing in all his glory, Shiva asked Bhagirath, 'What is it that you desire?'

Bhagirath fell at Shiva's feet. 'O lord, none but you can withstand the force of Ganga's descent from heaven. Please receive her, I beg of you, so she can go to paataal and water the ashes of my forefathers so that their souls can ascend to heaven.'

'So be it,' said the great Shiva. 'I shall receive Ganga on my head before she touches the earth and proceeds to paataal. May her grace be upon you.'

Once Shiva had promised help to Bhagirath, the safety of the earth was assured. There was no longer any fear of the earth being washed away by the force of the river's descent. But Ganga was no ordinary river. Beautiful beyond description, beloved of the gods, held in the greatest possible esteem by men, Ganga had become arrogant. She thought she would fall on the head of Shiva and sweep away the great god himself to paataal.

But Shiva decided to teach Ganga a lesson. The flood waters of Ganga fell on Shiva's head, heaving and swirling, but the tangle of Shiva's matted hair would not permit even a drop to escape. Ganga tossed and turned with all her might but she was held firmly in position, a prisoner.

No doubt this was a lesson to Ganga. But it was a bitter disappointment to Bhagirath who had gone to so much trouble to bring Ganga this far. But Bhagirath was not one to give up. He began his penance all over again, to please Shiva. In time Shiva took pity on him and gently let out the waters of Ganga. The waters divided into seven streams as they fell. Three of them flowed west and three east. The seventh followed Bhagirath who led the way. He was beside himself with joy to think that his ancestors would finally achieve salvation.

Bhagirath drove a chariot, grand as only a king's chariot could be. And Ganga came after, her waters rippling and dancing as she carved out a path for herself. Fast or slow, leaping over cliffs and gliding over plains, Ganga went where Bhagirath took her. And it was such a beautiful sight that even the gods in heaven gathered to witness it.

Bhagirath took Ganga to the ocean and from there all the way to paataal. With the holy waters Bhagirath performed the funeral rites for his ancestors and their souls rose to heaven. Since it was Bhagirath who succeeded in bringing the river down to earth, Ganga is also known as Bhagirathi. And it is considered sacred because it came from heaven.

Ganapati and Kuber

The Puranas are ancient books, eighteen in number. They are a collection of old, traditional stories, mainly devoted to the three most powerful Hindu gods—Brahma, Vishnu and Mahesh (Shiva). But other gods and goddesses also figure in these stories. So do kings, princes and heroes.

The following is a story from the Puranas. It centres around Ganapati (Ganesh), the son of Lord Shiva. Ganapati is believed to be short and plump, with the head of an elephant and the body of a man. Cheerful by nature, Ganapati is the god of wisdom and good beginnings. He is said to remove obstacles from the path of a devotee. That is why, before starting anything new, people pray to Ganapati and seek his blessings.

Kuber was the god of wealth. He was the owner of all the precious metals like gold and silver and all the gems like diamonds, rubies and emeralds found under the surface of the earth. Naturally, Kuber was very, very rich. He was richest of all the gods and richer than any man on earth.

Sad to say, all these riches had made Kuber very proud. He had only one desire—to show off his wealth so that people should be impressed by him. Kuber displayed his wealth by building grand palaces and by throwing grand feasts to which thousands of people were invited. He gave lavish gifts to kings and princes. He also gave freely in charity to the poor. And when people talked about his great wealth or praised the grand style in which he lived, he was very happy. Strangely enough, Kuber's wealth kept increasing all the time. He spent it night and day but it only kept growing. That is because he was a devotee of Lord Shiva. Pleased with his worship, Lord Shiva had granted him this boon.

Once it occurred to Kuber that he should invite all the gods in heaven to a feast. Since he was a devotee of Shiva, he thought of inviting Shiva first of all. Kuber did not lose much time thinking about it. He mounted his golden chariot and promptly went to Mount Kailash, which was the abode of Lord Shiva.

Kuber bowed before Lord Shiva and touched his feet. 'O greatest of the great,' said he, 'how can I ever thank you enough for all that you have given me? Whatever I have today is a boon from you. If you had not been so kind, where would Kuber be today?'

'I have heard all that before,' said Lord Shiva with a smile. 'Now tell me the real reason why you came here.'

'O lord,' said Kuber, 'I have come to invite you to a feast at my place. I wish to make it a truly grand feast, the like of which nobody has ever seen before. Will you please do me the honour of accepting my invitation?'

Lord Shiva smiled and said, 'My dear Kuber, leave me out of all this. I am not in the habit of attending feasts.'

'Take pity on me, O lord,' begged Kuber. 'Don't turn down my request. I have come all this way specially to invite you. . . Oh all right, if you really do not wish to come, please permit me to invite Goddess Parvati (Lord Shiva's wife) and the children.'

Lord Shiva replied, 'If I don't go, my wife will not go either. As for the children, can you imagine them going anywhere without their mother?'

Now Kuber was getting really desperate. He fell at Shiva's feet. 'My lord,' he cried, 'if nobody from your family comes to the feast, it will be a real disgrace for me. Before coming here I had announced with great pride that I was going to Mount Kailash to invite you. Now everyone will make fun of me.'

Lord Shiva thought for a moment and said, 'There's only one way out. I shall send my little son Ganapati to attend your feast.' And with that Kuber had to be content. It was certainly not what he had in mind. He had wished to invite the great Lord Shiva

himself, so that everyone would talk about it for all time to come. But Ganapati? Oh no! He was still too small to be of much importance. Anyway, this was the best that could be done. So Kuber fixed a day for the feast, touched Lord Shiva's feet and came away.

Back home, Kuber plunged into preparations for the feast of a lifetime. He wished to outdo both gods and human beings. The feast had to be made unforgettable so that the name of Kuber was covered with everlasting glory.

Since money was no problem, Kuber did things on a grand scale. He ordered the royal masons to build a massive hall, large enough to seat ten thousand guests. He also told them to build ten new kitchens. Each kitchen was to be spacious enough for twenty-five cooks and their helpers to work in together. The royal goldsmiths and silversmiths were told to make brand new vessels of gold and silver for the guests to eat from. And the royal stores were filled to bursting with grain, ghee, spices and the choicest vegetables, fruit and nuts from all over heaven and earth. Kuber made sure he would have the best of everything and plenty of it too. After all, it was no joke. He had invited at one go all the gods and goddesses in heaven and all the rajas and maharajas on earth along with their families and friends!

At last the great day arrived. Dressed in shimmering silks and brocades and covered with jewels, the guests began to pour in. They were welcomed at the ceremonial gate by Kuber and his family. Soon all the guests were seated. But the feast could not begin till Lord Shiva's son Ganapati had arrived.

Ganapati came at a run. Nodding to Kuber and his family he declared, 'I'm hungry. Where's the food?'

'This way, Maharaj,' said Kuber, smiling at his little guest. He led Ganapati to the hall which shone in the light of a thousand lamps. He offered Ganapati a golden mat to sit on. There were mounds of fruit on either side of Ganapati. And attendants ran to place before him gold platters full of fifty-six different dishes prepared with the utmost care by a team of expert cooks.

Ganapati sat down cross-legged on the mat and began to eat. And the food began to disappear at top speed. Kuber was watching. When a few morsels were still left, Ganapati was served a second and much larger helping. This also he finished in no time. A third helping followed and met with the same fate. The moment anything was served, it was finished. If there was even the slightest delay, Ganapati would burst into loud complaints. Kuber was getting nervous. He ordered the attendants to go on piling food before Ganapati constantly, without a break. The attendants got worn out serving him but Ganapati did not get worn out eating. In a short while he had finished all the food meant for thousands of people. But he was still hungry.

Kuber was now in a panic. He ordered his cooks to prepare more food. But Ganapati wouldn't stand any delay. 'I want food,' he said. 'And I want it now! I'm hungry!' And with this he marched off towards Kuber's palace. Kuber dashed after him.

Inside the palace Ganapati made straight for the kitchen and finished all the food that he could lay his hands on. Then he marched from room to room, looking for more. In the end he stood at the palace gate and told Kuber, 'Why did you invite me to your place at all? You didn't even have enough food for me. I'm going to complain to my father that you never gave me enough to eat.'

There were many other people standing nearby and they all heard what Ganapati said. Kuber was covered with shame. What would people think of him? He had the cheek to invite Ganapati himself and did not even feed him properly! But there was no time to think of all this. Ganapati had already set out for Mount Kailash and Kuber had to dash after him.

They found Lord Shiva seated on a snow-covered rock. Kuber fell at his feet. 'What's the matter?' asked Lord Shiva.

Ganapati pulled a face, pointing a finger at Kuber. 'This man invited me to a feast but didn't even give me enough to eat! I'm telling you Father, I'm still hungry.'

Lord Shiva smiled. 'Go in then and ask your mother to give you something to eat.' Ganapati went in. 'My dear Kuber,' said Lord Shiva, 'do come and sit down.' But Kuber covered his face with both hands. He had been disgraced in front of thousands of people but he knew he deserved it. He had become too proud. Didn't he wish to show off to everyone that he was rich and important and a special favourite of the great Lord Shiva?

Ashamed of his folly, Kuber fell at the feet of Lord Shiva and begged to be forgiven.

The Thirteenth Year

The following legend comes from the great epic Mahabharat.
The Mahabharat is the history of the Kuru dynasty which
ruled from Hastinapur in north India. The Kauravas and
the Pandavas were cousins and princes of Kuru dynasty.
The Kauravas were evil men and terribly jealous of the
Pandavas, who were not only noble but also very talented.
Duryodhan, the eldest of the Kauravas, invited Yudhishtir,
the eldest of the Pandavas, to a game of dice. Using foul
means, Duryodhan defeated Yudhishtir. As a forfeit
Yudhishtir, his four brothers and wife Draupadi were
banished to the forest for twelve years. As if this were not
enough, they were to spend the thirteenth year in disguise. If
they were discovered, they would have to spend another
twelve years in the forest. The following story relates what
happened in the thirteenth year.

*

Time passed slowly for the Pandavas in the forest. They kept
themselves busy in prayer, meditation and religious sacrifices.
They listened to the discourses of the learned brahmins who had
accompanied them. And a lot of time was spent fighting the
dangerous animals and demons who roamed about freely. It was
a hard life. But at last the twelve-year period was over. And now a
bigger problem stared them in the face. They were to spend the
thirteenth year in disguise, so that nobody could recognize them.
If they were recognized, they would have to spend another twelve
years in the forest, as punishment.

To live in disguise was going to be very difficult as Duryodhan's
spies were everywhere, scattered through the forest and in

neighbouring kingdoms. It would be almost impossible for the Pandavas to hide from their keen eyes. Besides, the Pandavas were five brothers in all and Draupadi always went with them. They wished to be together, which was only natural. But then it also posed a danger. A group of five men and one woman was very easy to spot. So living in the forest was out of the question. They would have to move to a city and mingle with the crowds.

After much thought and discussion, the Pandavas decided to spend the thirteenth year in the kingdom known as Matsya. The ruler of Matsya, King Virat, was a noble and upright man. He had always been a friend of the Pandavas and heartily disliked Duryodhan. The Pandavas had every hope that Virat would not be able to see through their disguise. But, even if he did, he would not report the matter to Duryodhan. Thus the Pandavas could feel reasonably safe and secure in the kingdom of Matsya.

The Pandavas took up service under King Virat. Yudhishtir donned the garb of an ascetic and became one of Virat's courtiers. The next brother Bhim took service as the royal cook for he not only cooked well but also had a big appetite. Arjun, the third Pandava, was an expert singer and dancer. He disguised himself as a woman and took up teaching singing and dancing to the ladies at Virat's court. Nakul, the fourth brother, had a great love for horses so he took service in the royal stables. The youngest brother Sahdev took a job tending Virat's cows because he knew how to look after cows. The beautiful, graceful Draupadi, herself a princess, became a sairandhari, companion and attendant, to Virat's queen Sudeshna.

For a few months all went well. But trouble was already brewing. Queen Sudeshna had a brother named Kichak, who was the commander-in-chief of Virat's army. Kichak was very brave and strong, but he was also very proud of his strength. If he wanted something, he simply took it by force. One day Kichak happened to see Draupadi. She was so beautiful that he immediately fell in love with her and wanted to marry her. Draupadi refused his advances and tried her best to rebuff him. But Kichak was not one to be put off so easily. He continued to harass Draupadi, demanding repeatedly that she must marry him. Tired of Kichak's behaviour, Draupadi at last reported the matter to Bhim. Bhim had a temper to match his strength. He had a fight with Kichak and killed him.

The people of Matsya were shocked to hear of Kichak's death. 'Who could have killed such a strong man?' they asked. 'And why?' But nobody could find a clue. In due course the news reached the ears of Duryodhan. Cunning that he was, he began to think, 'Kichak was too strong to be killed by anyone except Bhim. I'm sure Bhim is at the back of all this and the Pandavas were hiding in the kingdom of Virat. Now if only I could rip off their disguise, they would be forced to go back to the forest for another twelve years and I would be rid of them. . . But how can I possibly do that? I can't ask Virat for help. He has always been against us. . . .'

Duryodhan thought hard and finally hit upon a plan. He told his ministers, 'I suspect that the Pandavas are in Virat's kingdom. It would be a good thing to invade Matsya now and carry away the king's cows. Virat has been considerably weakened by the death of Kichak. When we attack, the Pandavas will surely come to his help in order to repay his hospitality. We'll spot them immediately and send them to the forest for another twelve years. Even if the Pandavas are not in Virat's kingdom, we lose nothing by invading it. In fact, it will provide us with a bit of sport.'

A neighbouring king, Susharma by name, supported this plan. It was decided that Susharma should attack Matsya from the south and seize the king's cattle. Virat would naturally send his army to the south. Just then Duryodhan would launch an attack from the north, which would be undefended. With both south and north under attack from enemy forces, the Pandavas would have to come out into the open so as to help Virat. And that would be the end as far as the Pandavas were concerned.

Susharma invaded Matsya from the south, as planned. He seized the cattle on the royal farms and laid waste all the fields and the orchards on the way. The cowherds ran to Virat with an appeal for help. The king very much wished that Kichak were alive, for he would have known how to deal with the enemy. But with Kichak gone, Virat was at a loss what to do.

At that very moment Yudhishtir came forward with an offer of help. He said, 'O king, though I am an ascetic, yet I am an expert at the art of warfare. Three other men in your service are also great fighters—your cook, your stable-keeper and your cowherd. I know this because we have all learnt the skills of warfare under the great Pandavas.'

'Is that so?' asked Virat, delighted with the news. 'Does that mean you will help me against the enemy?'

'Most certainly,' replied Yudhishtir. 'In fact, we are eager to do so. Please arrange for chariots to take us to the battle-front. We shall also need weapons, the sharpest that you have in your armoury.'

Virat was only too happy to accept the offer. Strengthened by the presence of the Pandava brothers, Virat's army marched in splendid formation to meet the enemy. A fierce battle followed, with much loss of lives on both sides. But in the end Susharma's army was defeated.

News of Susharma's defeat reached the city and the people went wild with joy. They began to make grand preparations to receive the king. But their joy was short-lived, for just then news arrived that Duryodhan had attacked Matsya from the north. He was at the head of a large army and was plundering orchards and farms and rounding up the hundreds of cows that lived on these farms.

Once again the cowherds ran to the king's palace. The king was away fighting in the south. So the cowherds went to his son Prince Uttaran. 'O prince, please save us,' they cried. 'The Kaurava army has invaded Matsya and is robbing as of our cows. In the absence of King Virat, you are the only one who can help us. O brave prince, come and save us and uphold the honour of your family.'

Prince Uttaran was still young and had little experience of warfare. So he fell for all this flattery. It went straight to his head and he began to brag, 'Indeed I can save this kingdom from the enemy and recover all those cows single-handed! Wait till you see me in action. I'm no less than Arjun himself, the greatest of great warriors! The only trouble is, all the best men have gone to battle. I have nobody to act as my charioteer so that I could go to the field of battle and strike terror into the hearts of the enemy. ' And Uttaran strutted up and down the room, twirling a moustache that was hardly there.

Draupadi heard Uttaran and laughed at the way he was bragging. To think that he compared himself with no less a warrior than Arjun! He must be very ignorant indeed!

Draupadi knew that war was a serious business. She also knew that Uttaran would not be able to cope with the highly skilled and powerful Kaurava army under Duryodhan. She wished to help. But being only a sairandhari, she could not talk directly to the prince. Court etiquette would not permit it. So Draupadi ran to Uttaran's sister, Princess Uttara, and told her about the Kaurava attack from the north. The princess was alarmed. 'What shall we do now?' she asked,

'That's no problem,' said Draupadi confidently. She dropped her voice and whispered in the princess's ear, 'Believe it or not, your music teacher has been the charioteer of Arjun himself! When. I was in the service of Draupadi, I heard of it.'

'What? How is that possible?' cried Uttara.

'Oh, but it is, I can assure you. What is more, this music teacher has also learnt archery from Arjun himself. O princess, if you have the welfare of Matsya at heart, order this music teacher to drive the prince's chariot to battle.'

Draupadi went to Uttara and Uttara went to Uttaran. And after much debate and discussion, it was settled that the music teacher should drive the prince's chariot.

Now it was Arjun's turn to put on an act. Hair braided, head covered with a chadar, always trying to hide his impressive height and physique behind voluminous clothes, poor Arjun had had enough of playing a woman. Here was a possibility of some action. He was delighted. But he had to be careful. Nothing must give away his identity. So when the prince asked him to be his charioteer, Arjun pretended to be horrified. He threw up his hands and said in a squeaky voice, 'Who, me? Never! What do I know of driving chariots?' And he hid his face as though overcome by shyness.

But the prince would not take no for an answer. Neither would the princess and her handmaidens. In the end Arjun agreed to their request, on condition that Prince Uttaran should protect 'her' on the field of battle. Arjun picked up the weapons provided for him, bungling a little so as to raise a laugh among the women and to allay suspicion, if any. At long last, Uttaran was in the chariot, with Arjun holding the reins in his hands. The horses understood that the charioteer was no ordinary man. They flew at his command and the chariot sped northwards.

At first Prince Uttaran kept urging Arjun to go faster and faster. But the moment he saw the Kaurava army, his heart sank. The Kauravas had all their stalwarts standing in battle array—Bhishma, Dronacharya, Kripacharya, Duryodhan and Karna. It was a galaxy of warriors and Uttaran knew they would soon reduce him to pulp. He began to shake with fear. 'O charioteer,' he begged, 'please let us go back. Never mind what people think of me. Let them laugh, if they so wish. But I can't possibly face all those fearsome warriors alone. Please, please let us turn back!'

At this Arjun smiled. 'What, O prince? Scared so soon? And all this time you were itching for a fight! Come, we must show the enemy that we are made of stern stuff and nothing can frighten us! Fight for the honour and glory of your family!'

But the prince was scared out of his wits. When Arjun refused to turn the chariot back, Uttaran leapt over the side and ran for dear life. But Arjun was too quick for him. Bidding the horses stand still, Arjun dashed after Uttaran and hauled him back to the chariot. Once again he began to reason with the terrified prince.

From his place in the Kaurava ranks, Dronacharya saw all this and he became suspicious. He thought, 'That charioteer is wearing a woman's clothes all right, but he can't possibly be a woman. He is much too tall and powerfully built. Could it be Arjun?' Drona shared his views with the others and they became suspicious too.

Meanwhile Arjun had changed his tactics in dealing with Uttaran. He was speaking kindly and trying to build up the prince's confidence. 'Don't be afraid,' he comforted Uttaran. 'I'm here to fight the Kauravas. Tell you what, you drive the chariot and I shall do the fighting.' With that, Arjun put the reins into Uttaran's hands and told him to drive the chariot to a tree near the cremation ground.

At the very mention of the tree, Uttaran turned pale. 'No no, not that tree,' he cried. 'There's a bundle hanging from one of the branches and people say it contains the corpse of an old huntress!'

'It's not a corpse, I tell you,' said Arjun sternly. 'That bundle contains the weapons of the Pandavas. Do as I say.'

Seeing that he had no choice, Uttaran climbed up the tree and brought the bundle down. When he opened it, he saw weapons as bright as the sun. Uttaran was amazed. 'O charioteer, what a marvel this is! These weapons really look as though they belong to heroes like the Pandavas. But the Pandavas have been deprived of their kingdom and banished to the forest. Do you know them? Where are they now?'

At this Arjun told Uttaran how all five Pandavas and Draupadi had taken up service at Virat's court. He also told the prince who he really was. Uttaran was completely floored by the presence of Arjun, the mighty warrior. 'How fortunate I am to be able to see you with my own eyes! Meeting you has put great courage into me,' he said with folded hands.

Arjun spoke words of encouragement. He was a great warrior but he never looked down on people less brave than himself. He smiled at Uttaran. 'Have no fear, O prince. You will soon see me defeat the Kauravas and recover the cows.'

Arjun's chariot thundered on its way, seeming to shake the very earth. The hearts of the Kauravas quaked with fear when they heard the twang of Arjun's bowstring. Duryodhan hated the sound. But he also took it as a message of hope. To Dronacharya he said, 'The Pandavas had pledged to spend twelve years in the forest and one year in disguise. The thirteenth year is not yet over and Arjun has been discovered. Now the Pandavas will have to go back to the forest for another twelve years.'

But their patriarch Bhishma held up his hand. 'Duryodhan, your calculation is wrong. The thirteenth year ended yesterday. Arjun would not have revealed himself otherwise. Now he has every right to come forward and give us battle. We had better prepare ourselves.'

Everyone agreed. Dronacharya, the master of military strategy, already had a plan. He said, 'Let us divide our army into four parts. Duryodhan can take one part to guard him on his way and return to Hastinapur. Another part can surround the cows and seize them. With the remaining two parts we shall fight Arjun.'

The Kaurava forces arranged themselves accordingly. But Arjun had not come to fight them. He had come to recover the cows belonging to Virat and to save the honour of Matsya. He also had a score to settle with his arch-enemy Duryodhan. For this reason Arjun moved away from the Kaurava forces and went in hot pursuit of the soldiers who had seized the cows. But in passing he shot three arrows that fell at the feet of Bhishma, Drona and Kripa. It was Arjun's way of touching the feet of his grandsire and his teachers.

Arjun easily defeated the enemy and brought back the cows. He then restored them to the cowherds and set off after Duryodhan. A fierce battle followed. Arjun defeated Duryodhan and put him to flight. But when Arjun accused him of being a coward, Duryodhan turned back and the battle that followed was far more fierce than the one before. Arjun fought hard and finally used a divine weapon so that all the Kauravas fell unconscious on the battlefield. As a sign of a decisive victory, Arjun snatched away their upper garments. He then drove Prince Uttaran back to the city.

When the news of Uttaran's victory reached Matsya, there was great rejoicing. King Virat had arrived back in the meantime and his excitement knew no bounds. Proud of his son's achievement, he decided to receive Uttaran in court with all the honour due to a hero.

When the court was assembled, King Virat walked in. But what was this? Seated in places of honour, reserved for princes, were men of little importance, the ascetic, the cook and keepers of the royal horses and cows. Virat lost his temper. 'What is the meaning of this?' he thundered. 'So what if you helped us fight the army of Susharma? That does not entitle you to such high positions at court!'

The Pandavas smiled, and this made the king even more angry. He was still fuming when who should walk in but Prince Uttaran. Virat was beside himself with joy. He embraced his son. 'I'm proud of you, my boy,' he said. 'You are indeed a hero! How did you manage to defeat the powerful Kaurava army and recover the cows?'

Prince Uttaran hung his head in embarrassment. 'Father,' he said. 'I conquered no army and recovered no cows. It was the work of the Pandava prince Arjun. He guided me to the field of battle and fought to win the day. All the honour should go to him.'

Virat was amazed. 'Arjun, the Pandava prince!' he cried. 'Where is he? How come a Pandava is living in my kingdom and I know nothing about it?'

The Pandava brothers now realized that they had had enough fun at Virat's expense. Yudhishtir rose in his seat, followed by Bhim, Nakul and Sahdev, even as Arjun entered through the ornamental gate. 'O king,' said Yudhishtir, we are the five Pandavas. Have no doubt about that. And please accept our grateful thanks for providing us with a home this past one year.'

King Virat realized with a shock that the men he had just pulled up for taking seats of honour were really the famous Pandavas. He begged them to forgive him and offered them his entire kingdom and all his treasure as a gift. But of course the Pandavas were not willing to take anything. Finally it was decided that Princess Uttara be given in marriage to Arjun's son Abhimanyu. In due course the Pandavas left the kingdom of Matsya. They were given a fond farewell by King Virat, Prince Uttaran and the people of Matsya. And thus, in a burst of glory, ended the thirteenth year of the Pandavas' exile.

When all these events took place, Prince Uttaran was still a youth. Growing to manhood, he fought valiantly for the Pandavas in the battle of Mahabharat and gave up his life on the battlefield.

Ram and the Squirrel

Here is a story woven around Ram, the central figure in the famous epic Ramayan. Ram is so well loved that stories about him have been told and retold for centuries. But they are still popular.

Ram was a prince of the kingdom of Kosala, which had its capital at Ayodhya. His father, King Dasharath, had three wives. Ram was the son of the eldest wife, Kaushalya. He had three younger brothers. Being the eldest of the brothers, Ram was heir to the throne. At the proper time King Dasharath decided to step down from the throne. He announced the day of Ram's coronation. The announcement was greeted with tremendous joy by the people of Ayodhya because they all loved Ram. But the day before the coronation Dasharath's youngest queen Kaikeyi and her maid Manthara hatched a wicked plot against Ram. As a result, Ram was not only deprived of his throne, he was also banished to the forest for fourteen long years. The following is an account of something that happened during these fourteen years.

*

Banished from Ayodhya, Ram left for the forest. His wife Sita and his brother Lakshman went with him. They made a hut for themselves and began to live in it. The forest was full of wild animals. But even more dangerous than these were the rakshasas who roamed about freely and killed human beings for sport. These demons could change their shape and appearance at will. One day Ram and Lakshman were both away and Sita was alone. Ravan, the rakshasa king of Lanka, came to the hut disguised as a sadhu. The moment Sita came out of the hut to give him alms, Ravan caught hold of her, mounted his flying chariot and flew away to his kingdom across the sea.

Ram and Lakshman came back to the hut to find Sita missing. They hunted for her everywhere but she was nowhere to be found. Ram was overwhelmed by grief. He wandered through the forest, asking every single living being if anyone had seen his beloved Sita. Lakshman was a great help and support to his brother. But there was little he could do to help Ram, so great was Ram's sorrow.

At length Ram and Lakshman met Jatayu, king of the eagles. Jatayu told them that Sita had been carried away by the rakshasa king Ravan in his flying chariot. Jatayu was very pious and god-fearing. He was also a close friend of Ram's father, King Dasharath. Distressed by Sita's plight, he had fought Ravan with all his might. But Ravan proved too strong for him. Jatayu was mortally wounded. He lived just long enough to tell Ram what he had seen. Then he closed his eyes and died.

Ram and Lakshman set out again in search of Sita. At last they came to Rishyamook hill. The monkey king Sugreev lived on this hill, with a band of his faithful followers. A great friendship developed between Sugreev and Ram. Sugreev told Ram, 'Some days ago I saw a beautiful woman being carried away by a dreadful demon. He looked like Ravan, the king of Lanka. As the demon tore across the sky, the lady saw us. She took off all her jewels, tied them up in a piece of cloth and threw the bundle down. We picked up the bundle. See if the jewels belong to Sita.'

Ram saw the jewels and anguish filled his soul. The jewels did belong to Sita. Where was she and in what condition? How was the rakshasa treating her? Ram's eyes filled with tears. Sugreev saw Ram's grief. He and his faithful followers vowed to help Ram against Ravan and to bring back Sita.

Sugreev gathered his army under his great general Hanuman. The army consisted of hordes of monkeys and bears, each stronger than the other. They all marched down to the sea, beyond which lay the kingdom of Lanka. They had to cross the sea in order to reach Lanka.

Ram began to shoot arrows into the sea. He wished to control the sea and force it to make way for the army to pass through. The arrows were so powerful and produced so much heat that the water began to hiss. All the creatures who lived in the water began to fear for their lives. And they appealed to the god of the sea to help them.

The sea god appeared before Ram. He said, 'Do not shoot arrows into my kingdom, O prince. You cannot overcome the sea in this manner. If you wish to cross the sea, you must build a bridge over it. In the army of Sugreev you have the son of Vishwakarma himself. Vishwakarma is the engineer of the gods and his son is called Nala. He has the ability to build the bridge. Ask him to do so. Ask the monkeys and the bears to help by bringing boulders and trees. And I shall help by receiving these things and keeping them in place in the water.' With these words the sea god disappeared. Ram told Sugreev what the sea god had told him and Sugreev in turn ordered Nala to build a bridge.

Soon hundreds and thousands monkeys and bears had spread out all over the mountains and forests. They uprooted trees and rolled down rocks from the mountains. They dragged both the trees and the rocks to the shore and threw these into the sea. The water splashed high. Standing by the seashore, Nala supervised the work. Day after day the work went on, amid great noise and confusion. Ram's heart filled with joy to see the army of monkeys and bears working so willingly to build the massive bridge. One day while the work was in progress, a small brown squirrel came running to the shore. She was carrying little pebbles in her mouth. She placed the pebbles alongside the great boulders and ran back for more. Back and forth, back and forth she went till some of the monkeys saw her. 'What!' they laughed, 'this chit of a creature actually thinks she's helping us! Fancy bringing little pebbles to build a giant bridge like this!' The bears joined in their merriment. In fact, one of them tried to catch hold of the squirrel but she was too quick for him.

Dodging the bears and the monkeys who made fun of her, the little squirrel ran straight to Ram. She found him talking to Nala. He was too tall for her so she stood on her haunches and spoke as loud as she could. 'Look at all those horrid bears and monkeys,' she said. 'They are making fun of me. Tell them to stop. I also want to help build a bridge so you can cross over to Lanka and bring back Sita Ma.'

Ram heard the squirrel's voice above the roar of the sea and the noise of bridge building. He bent forward and lifted up the squirrel between his two palms. His heart melted to see that she had tears in her eyes. 'Little one,' he said, 'I'm very grateful to you for your help. Run along and do your bit. The bridge will be made stronger by the pebbles that you bring. And nobody will make fun of you anymore!'

Ram gently stroked the squirrel's back with his fingers. When he raised his hand, the marks of his fingers were there, white against the brown fur. And ever since then the squirrel has carried three white stripes on her back, as a token of Ram's affection.

In due course the bridge was completed. Ram and Lakshman crossed over with Sugreev's army led by Hanuman. A great battle followed. Ravan was killed and Sita finally restored to Ram. They came back to Ayodhya and were received with great joy by the people. King Dasharath had died in the meantime so Ram ascended the throne and ruled for many years.

The God Ayyappan

In Kerala there is a hill known as Sabarimala (Hill of Sabari). Sabari was a woman rishi who is believed to have lived on this very hill. It was here that she had the great good fortune of meeting Lord Ram as he wandered from place to place during his search for his wife Sita.

On Sabarimala stands the temple of Ayyappan. He is perhaps the most popular of all the gods worshipped in Kerala. Every year, on the festival of Makar Sankranti, thousands of pilgrims go to this temple to worship Ayyappan. At one time the forest on Sabarimala was full of wild animals, but this did not keep away the worshippers. Here is an account of the years that Ayyappan spent on earth.

*

A long, long time ago there lived a female demon called Mahishi. So wicked and cruel was she that everyone dreaded her. She killed people for no reason and destroyed their homes and crops. Anyone who came to slay her got killed instead. In time even the lesser gods began to fear Mahishi. So they prayed to the two mightiest gods Hari and Hara (Vishnu and Shiva) to save the world from her clutches. And the two gods promised that they would create a child who would grow up and slay Mahishi.

Some time later King Rajashekhara of Panthalam went out on a hunt. He rode deep into the forest in search of game. There, to his utter surprise, he found a baby boy lying on the ground. The king could see that this was no ordinary baby. His little body seemed to glow with a soft light and around his neck he wore a golden bell. Now the king had no children of his own and had often prayed for a son. He thought this baby was an answer to his prayers. Delighted, he picked up the child and brought it home.

The king and queen both loved the child dearly. They named him Manikanthan. (He is better known as Ayyappan.) The baby grew up in the palace and was the pride and joy of his foster parents.

But Ayyappan's good days did not last. A few years later the queen gave birth to a boy. And soon after that, her feelings for her adopted son began to change. She no longer loved Ayyappan as before. In fact she grew jealous of the king's love for the boy. She hated to think that one day Ayyappan would sit on the throne and not her own son. Her dislike for Ayyappan grew so strong that she could no longer stand the sight of him. So she decided to have him killed.

Some of the ministers at court did not like Ayyappan either. Even they were jealous of the king's affection for the boy. Now the queen and these ministers hatched a plot to send Ayyappan to his death. So clever was the plot that nobody could even suspect the queen to have a hand in it.

In keeping with the wicked plan, the queen suddenly began to pretend that she was very ill. The physician who came to treat her was one of the plotters too. He had been bribed to tell a lie. So he examined the queen and declared that she was suffering from a terrible disease.

The king was shocked. He loved his wife very much. 'Is there no treatment for this disease?' he asked. 'Surely you know of *some* remedy?'

'There is a remedy,' came the reply. 'But it is so difficult to obtain that it's futile even to think about it.'

'What is it?' cried the king. 'Just tell me. I'll do anything to make the queen well again.'

The physician pretended to hesitate. Finally he announced, with a very serious face, 'The only remedy for the queen's ailment is the milk of a tigress.'

The king's hopes were dashed to the ground. 'Impossible!' he sighed. 'This is impossible! I don't think there's anybody in my kingdom brave enough to get the milk of a tigress.'

From her bed the wicked queen moaned, 'Alas, then there is no hope for me.'

The king was desperate. He announced that anyone who could bring the milk of a tigress would get a reward far beyond his wildest dreams. A few brave men tried and lost their lives. It did seem there was no hope for the queen when one day Ayyappan told the king that he would try to get the remedy needed by his mother.

The king was not ready to lose his precious son. 'How can you even attempt such a thing?' he cried. 'You are only twelve years old! Several people have lost their lives trying, and they were much older and stronger than you.' But Ayyappan had made up his mind. He also insisted on going alone, without a bodyguard.

Armed with nothing but a bow and arrow, Ayyappan went into the forest. The terrible demon Mahishi saw him and came charging at him. But one arrow from Ayyappan's bow and she lay dead. Ayyappan pressed on, in search of a tigress.

That evening, around sunset, the people of Panthalam heard a sound the like of which they had never heard before. Hundreds of tigers were roaring all at once. Men and women rushed out of their homes. The king and his courtiers rushed to the roof of the palace. Even the queen forgot her pretended illness and ran to her balcony. What they saw was terrifying. Ayyappan was riding into town on the back of a tigress. And following behind were hundreds of other tigers.

The people were awestruck. 'Our Ayyappan is no ordinary mortal,' they cried. 'He is a god!' The king's heart was bursting with pride and joy. 'My son,' he said, 'how blessed we are to have you with us!' Ayyappan smiled. At the king's request he waved his hand and the roaring stopped. And then, to the utter amazement of the people, all the tigers turned and quietly disappeared into the forest.

The queen and all the courtiers who had plotted against Ayyappan now fell at his feet. They begged forgiveness and repeatedly requested him to stay and be their king. But he refused to stay. He told them that he had come down to earth only to rid the world of Mahishi. Since he had accomplished that, it was time to return to heaven.

The king made one last request. 'My son, knowing that you are divine, I wish to make a temple dedicated to you. Where shall I build it?' At this Ayyappan took out an arrow from his quiver and told his father to build the temple wherever the arrow fell. He shot the arrow and it fell right on top of Sabarimala.

Ayyappan went to live on Sabarimala and in time a beautiful temple was built there. It is believed that the great sage Parasuram himself came down to earth disguised as a sculptor and gave the king an image of Ayyappan to place in the temple. The image was exquisitely carved. The moment the king set eyes on it, he knew it was not the work of an ordinary man. He fell at the sculptor's feet. Parasuram then revealed to the king who he really was. He also told the king to open the temple for worship on the day of Makar Sankranti.

The king did as he was told. On the appointed day Ayyappan was asked to light the lamp in the temple. As he did so, a strange and wonderful thing happened. The flame moved towards the image and finally entered it. There was a burst of light. The whole world lit up for a moment as Ayyappan entered the image and was lost to view. Ayyappan was never seen again. But to this day it is believed that on Makar Sankranti day, he himself lights the lamp in the temple. And that is the day when hundreds of devotees flock to the temple to worship him.

Dronacharya

Hundred of years ago, the Kuru dynasty ruled over the kingdom of Hastinapur in north India. Dhritarashtra and Pandu were princes of this dynasty. They were brothers. Pandu had five sons known as the Pandavas, Yudhishtir being the eldest. Dhritarashtra had as many as a hundred sons known as the Kauravas. Duryodhana was the eldest of the Kauravas.

As children, both the Kauravas and Pandavas stayed together in the palace of Hastinapur. They lived under the care of their grandsire Bhishma and renowned gurus like Kripacharya and Dronacharya. The story of Dronacharya comes to us from the famous epic Mahabharat.

*

Drona was the son of a brahmin named Bhardwaj. Those days it was customary for the sons of brahmins to make a detailed study of the Vedas. Living in his father's ashram, Drona completed his study not only of the Vedas but of several other holy books as well. When this was done, he turned his attention to the practice of archery. So hard did he work at it that in time he became a legendary archer.

There were several other students living at the ashram of Bhardwaj. They had come from far and near to study the different branches of learning. One of these students was Drupad, son of the king of Panchal. Drupad and Drona became the best of friends. They spent all their waking hours together, cleaning the hermitage, fetching wood and water, attending to the needs of their guru and studying the Vedas. At night they slept side by side and talked of the future that lay before them.

Drona was the son of a poor brahmin. He did not expect to inherit any wealth from his father. But Drupad was the son of a king and in time the throne would come to him. Drupad was impulsive by nature. In a burst of generosity he would often make tall promises to Drona. He would say, 'My friend, you will always share in my good fortune. Just you wait and see. When I ascend the throne, I shall straightaway give you half my kingdom and no less.'

The years at the ashram were soon over and the two boys drifted apart. Drona grew to manhood and married a sister of another learned brahmin, Kripa. A son was born to them and they named him Ashwatthama.

After he had married and got a child, a change came over Drona. All these years he had never cared for wealth. He was content with the simplest clothes and the simplest living. But he loved his wife and son so dearly that he wished to provide them with the best of everything. Naturally, the best could not be had without money, so Drona began to crave for wealth. All his efforts came to be bent towards acquiring wealth. But it was not so easy. A few years rolled by, with Drona still leading the life of a very learned but poor man. But he employed his time usefully by learning the art of warfare from experts. In time Drona became an acknowledged master of the military arts.

Meanwhile Drupad had ascended the throne of Panchal, following the death of his father. Drona thought of the wonderful times he and his friend Drupad had as boys in the ashram of Bhardwaj. He thought of shared lessons and laughter, their rambles through the forest and the stories they had told one another. Most of all Drona remembered Drupad's promise of sharing his good fortune, even to the extent of giving away half his kingdom to Drona.

Drona went to the court of Drupad. He was sure of receiving a warm welcome from his old friend. But he realized with a shock that Drupad the king was very different from Drupad the student. When Drona introduced himself as an old friend, Drupad's eyes blazed with anger. 'How dare you call yourself my friend?' he demanded. 'I am a king, and you a beggar, wandering about in search of a livelihood. What a fool you must be to imagine that a few years spent together at an ashram would make you my friend for life! Friendship can exist only between equals. Leave my palace at once and don't show me your face again!'

Thus Drona was turned out of the palace and the humiliation was more than he could bear. Anger raged in his heart like a fire that would not be put out. Then and there Drona vowed to punish the king for his arrogance and for treating so casually a sacred thing like friendship.

There was nothing to do but look for employment elsewhere. And Drona did just that. He made his way to Hastinapur, the capital of the Kuru dynasty. But by then he was weary of wandering from one place to another. At Hastinapur he spent a few quiet days in the house of his brother-in-law Kripa, who had become the teacher of the Kauravas and Pandavas and was known as Kripacharya (Kripa the teacher).

One day Drona went to the outskirts of the city on some business. There he saw some of the Kaurava and Pandava princes playing with a ball. Drona stopped to watch the fun. In the course of the game the ball rolled towards a well. As Yudhishtir leapt forward to grab the ball, a ring slipped from his finger and followed the ball into the well. The princes crowded around the well. They could see the ring clearly, shining at the bottom, but had no means of taking it out. Neither could they retrieve the ball. Their faces fell as they looked around them, not knowing what to do.

Drona noticed the disappointment on the faces of the princes and walked up to them with a smile. 'You are princes of the Kuru dynasty,' he said, 'and you can't do a simple thing like taking out that ball? Shall I do it for you?'

Drona plucked a blade of grass. Holding it before him he uttered a certain mantra and sent it flying into the well. The blade of grass sped forward with all the force of an arrow and lodged itself in the ball. Drona sent many more blades of grass in quick succession. They clung together to form a chain. Drona had only to pull at the chain to take out the ball.

The princes were amazed. Who could ever dream of taking out the ball with the help of a few blades of grass? This man must indeed be a wizard. They begged of him to take out the ring as well. Drona borrowed a bow, fixed an arrow to the string and sent it straight into the ring. The arrow curved back in its flight and brought the ring with it. With a smile Drona handed the ring back to Yudhishtir.

By now the princes were speechless. They bowed to Drona and said, 'O brahmin, we are indeed blessed to have met you. Who are you?'

But Drona would not tell them his name. He simply said. 'Go to your grandsire Bhishma. He will tell you who I am.'

The princes lost no time running to Bhishma. When they gave a detailed description of the remarkable feats performed by the brahmin, Bhishma knew that it could be none other than the master Drona. Bhishma had been on the lookout for a teacher to instruct the Kaurava and Pandava princes in the use of arms. His choice now fell on Drona. Bhishma sent for Drona, received him with great honour and employed him as instructor to the princes. Drona's hard days were over. He began to live in comfort. He moved in the company of royalty and was honoured for his skill with weapons. Most important of all, he was able to provide his wife and son with luxuries and this gave him great satisfaction. But he had not forgotten the insult heaped upon him by Drupad. Drona was only biding his time and waiting for an opportunity to take revenge.

The opportunity came when the Kaurava and Pandava princes had acquired mastery in the use of arms. It was time for them to render some service to the master in return for the instruction they had received. This was the custom and was known as guru dakshina. As a service to him, Drona sent Duryodhan and Karna to Panchal to capture Drupad and bring him a prisoner to Hastinapur. Karna and Duryodhan went willingly enough. They were brave men and they tried their best. But Drupad proved more than a match for them and they came back disappointed.

Drona next chose Arjun, the Pandava prince, for the difficult task. Arjun defeated Drupad in battle and brought him before Drona, bound in chains.

Drona greeted his royal prisoner with a smile. He said, 'O king, have no fear. Your life is very safe in my hands. In our boyhood we were great friends. But you chose to forget that friendship and turned me out of your palace saying that friendship was possible only between equals. Now you and I shall be equal. Through the efforts of my disciple Arjun, I have conquered your kingdom. It is mine. But I shall give you half of it and keep the other half for myself. Now I am no longer a wandering beggar before a king. We are both kings. Surely now I can renew my friendship with you?'

With these words Drona set Drupad at liberty, returned his entire kingdom and treated him as an honoured guest. But, sad to say, their friendship could not be revived. Two things had destroyed it—first Drupad's arrogance and later, Drona's desire for revenge. Drona and Drupad had both been humbled and neither could forget the blow to his pride. In this way two close friends were turned into sworn enemies and remained that way till the end. So much so, that in the battle of Mahabharat, it was the son of Drupad who killed Dronacharya!

A Gift of Flour

This is a little-known legend from the Mahabharat. After the fierce battle between the Kauravas and Pandavas at Kurukshetra, peace was restored at last. The Kauravas perished to a man. The eldest Pandava brother, Yudhishtir, ascended the throne of Hastinapur. He was a good king, fair and just and always ready to help those in need. It is believed that few could compare with Yudhishtir in generosity. But the following legend has something different to say.

*

Some time after Yudhishtir was crowned, he performed a horse sacrifice called aswamedha yagya. This sacrifice was performed by none but the most powerful kings. All the princes of the land were invited and the celebrations were organized on a splendid scale. Beautiful gifts were distributed among the brahmins, the poor and the destitute who had flocked to Hastinapur from different parts of the country. The pundits who performed the religious rites and the kings and princes who attended were all loaded with gifts. When the yagya was over, Yudhishtir and all his brothers had every reason to feel happy and satisfied over a job well done. But this was not to be.

Just before the vast assembly broke up, there suddenly appeared, right in the middle of the pavilion, a weasel. The weasel rolled on the ground and laughed aloud. The laugh sounded almost human and it seemed that the weasel was mocking the people present.

The very sight of the weasel alarmed the guests. The priests took it to be an evil omen, particularly because one side of the weasel's body shone like gold. It just did not seem natural. Dropping everything else the head priest asked the weasel, 'Who on earth are you and why have you disturbed this distinguished gathering?'

The weasel did not answer at once. It first turned around and took a good look at the princes and learned brahmins gathered in the pavilion. And then it began to speak, 'O princes and priests, listen to me. No doubt you believe that the yagya has been completed in splendid style. But your magnificent horse sacrifice and all the gifts made in that connection are less glorious than the humble gift of maize flour given by the poor brahmin of Kurukshetra. Don't be so conceited about it. That brahmin's sacrifice was far greater than yours!'

The gathering was amazed to hear human speech from the throat of a weasel. Many people were highly displeased that anyone should talk so rudely in the presence of the noble Yudhishtir and his guests. The head priest spoke again. 'In what way has the yagya been found wanting? The mantras (holy verses) were recited in strict observance of the law. No ceremony, no rite was omitted. Both gods and ancestors were duly honoured. All the guests were welcomed as befitted their station in life. Each one is going home richer than he came and completely satisfied. What more could a yagya achieve and how can you say that the sacrifice of anyone else was greater?'

The weasel laughed again and said, 'O brahmin, no doubt Yudhishtir is one of the greatest among kings and the aswamedha yagya that he performed was perfect in every detail. But what I said was also true. The sacrifice of the brahmin of Kurukshetra was greater. Now listen to the story.

'Long before the battle of Mahabharat was fought between the Kauravas and Pandavas at Kurukshetra, there lived in that city a brahmin. His family consisted of his wife, son and daughter-in-law. They were very poor and obtained their daily food by picking grain that had fallen in the fields after harvesting was over.

'For many years they lived in this manner. But then the land was hit by a severe drought. There was no rain for months on end. Rivers and wells ran dry. The soil in the fields cracked for lack of moisture. There was no sowing or harvesting and no grain scattered in the fields to be gathered by the brahmin and his family.

'For many days they starved. One day, after wandering in the blazing sun for hours on end, they managed to gather a small quantity of maize. They came home, roasted the maize and ground it into flour. Then they divided the flour into four equal portions and eagerly sat down to eat. Just then a man entered their house and said he was very hungry, "I haven't eaten anything for days," he said. "Can you spare me a little food?"

'Without a moment's hesitation the brahmin stood up. He welcomed the guest, bringing him water to wash his feet and making him comfortable. Then he placed his own share of the flour before the guest. "This isn't much," said he, "but if you would eat it, I shall feel honoured." The guest ate the flour with gusto and at the end of it he was still hungry. The brahmin realized that his guest was not satisfied but he did not know what to do.

'Just then the brahmin's wife said, "My lord, please give my portion of the flour to our honoured guest. If his hunger is satisfied, I shall feel very happy indeed." The brahmin did not like the idea because he was devoted to his wife and could not bear to see her go hungry. But she insisted and in the end the brahmin had to agree. He placed his wife's portion of the flour before the guest and urged him to eat it. The guest finished the flour in no time but he was still hungry. The brahmin noticed that the guest was still not satisfied. He looked about him helplessly but what else could he offer?

'Then the brahmin's son came forward. He said, "Dear father, please give my portion of the flour to our honoured guest. If his hunger is satisfied, I shall be very happy indeed." The brahmin did not like the idea because he was deeply attached to his son and could not bear to see him suffer. But the son insisted and in the end he had to agree. The guest took the son's portion of maize flour and ate it eagerly. But he was still hungry.

'Before the brahmin could say anything, his daughter-in-law came forward. She placed her share of the maize flour before the brahmin and said, "Dear father, please let our honoured guest have this as well. Nothing would make me happier than to see him satisfied." The brahmin hesitated, for he loved his daughter-in-law like his own child. But in the end he had to agree.

'The guest ate the daughter-in-law's portion of the flour and his face began to glow with satisfaction. He said. "Blessed are you for the hospitality that you have offered me! Who can give away food when he himself is dying of hunger? But you did just that. Your supreme sacrifice has earned all of you a place in heaven. Look, the chariot of the gods has come to take you there!"

'As he said this, the mysterious guest disappeared. At the same time the brahmin and his family saw a beautiful golden chariot come down from the sky. It stopped at their very door. They stepped in and flew straight to heaven.'

The story of the brahmin of Kurukshetra was over but the weasel continued, 'I happened to be living near the house of that brahmin so I caught the aroma of flour. It made my head turn to gold. Out of sheer joy I went and rolled in the flour that had fallen on the floor and one side of my body became gold too. I turned on the other side but there was no more flour left and that part of me is still as it was. I want my entire body to turn golden so I go around looking for a place where a truly great sacrifice has been made. I came here in the hope that the sacrifice of the great and noble Yudhishtir might come up to this high standard. But it did not. This yagya was not as splendid as the gift of flour that the brahmin made to his guest.'

With these words the weasel disappeared. But he had uttered words of rare wisdom. They left a deep impression on the minds of the people in the pavilion. And for a long time they remained seated, in perfect silence, thinking over what they had heard.

Agastya

We have hundreds of legends associated with the geographical features of our country—the oceans, mountain ranges, rivers and lakes. Very often a well known person is the central figure of these legends. The following legend is connected with the mountain range known as Vindhyachal. Its central figure is Agastya, one of the great sages who lived in ancient times.

*

Agastya was the son of Varun, god of the sea. From his earliest days he had lived the life of an ascetic, deep inside a forest. He wore the bark of trees and ate only wild roots and fruit. But he studied the Vedas with great singlemindedness. In time he became one of the most learned men in the country.

For a long time Agastya was content with his life. But then something happened to disturb his peace. He had a dream in which he saw the spirits of his ancestors wandering about restlessly in the air. Agastya asked them why they were not in heaven. 'You were good people while you lived on earth,' he told them, 'so now you should be residing in heaven amid peace and plenty. Why have you come back to earth?'

The spirits replied, 'We have come back to earth because we are worried. At present you offer sacrifices in our name and that ensures our peace in the other world. But what happens when you are no more? You are not married and have no son. Who will take over your duties to your ancestors after you are gone?'

The spirits went on, 'For our sake, get married, dear son. Raise a family so that we may have someone to remember us and do a son's duty by us.'

At this point Agastya suddenly woke up. He had never before wished to get married. But now, out of a sense of duty to his ancestors, he decided to take a wife.

By then Agastya had earned renown as a sage. People came to him from far and near to ask for boons. One such person was the king of the country of Vidarbha. He was childless and came to Agastya so that he coulld be blessed with a child. Agastya heard the king's request and sat in meditation for a long time. Finally he announced to the king, who was waiting anxiously, 'You shall become the father of a beautiful girl. And this girl should be given in marriage to me.'

The sage's prophecy came true. Soon after, the queen of Vidarbha gave birth to a girl who was named Lopamudra. With the passing years she grew into a maiden of such exquisite beauty that her fame spread among all the royal households of the country. But no prince dared ask for her hand in marriage because Agastya wanted her for his wife and the princes were afraid of Agastya.

A few years later, Agastya came to the court of Vidarbha and asked for the hand of Lopamudra in marriage. Now the king had promised that this would be done. But when the time came, he was most unwilling to do so. His daughter had been brought up in the lap of luxury. She was a beautiful, delicate girl. How would she adjust to the rough life of an ashram in the forest?

Lopamudra realized that something was wrong. She begged to be told the truth. And when she finally learnt the truth, she gladly agreed to marry the sage.

Naturally, her parents were surprised. But they were also greatly relieved, and, in due course, the marriage was celebrated. The time came for Lopamudra to go to the forest with her husband. Like any royal bride, she was dressed in fabulous silks and laden with priceless jewels. But such finery had no place in the life of an ascetic. Agastya told his wife to give it all away and she did so with a smile. Covering herself with a deerskin and garments made of bark, she gladly accompanied the sage to his ashram.

Agastya and Lopamudra spent many years in prayer and meditation at a place called Gangadwar. They were very happy together and there developed between them a strong and abiding love. But in course of time Lopamudra got tired of life in an ashram. She began to long for a home of her own and at least some of the luxuries that she enjoyed in her father's house. When she mentioned this to Agastya he smiled and said, 'But how can I provide you with these luxuries? I have no money. We are like beggars living in the forest.'

'But you have all the powers of a great yogi,' said Lopamudra. 'If you so wish, you can get the wealth of the whole world in a single moment.'

'That is so indeed,' replied the sage. 'But if I were to use my yogic powers to collect a trifling thing like wealth, my powers would soon be lost. And all the austerities that I have practised all these years would be reduced to nothing.'

'That must never happen,' returned Lopamudra with feeling. 'But other men go out to earn. And I would also like you to earn enough wealth for us to live in ease and comfort.'

In those days brahmins like Agastya imparted education to young boys. They performed religious ceremonies and gave spiritual guidance to kings and commoners alike. In return it was the duty of every citizen to look after the physical needs of brahmins. Thus there was no shame attached to a brahmin seeking alms. Agastya now set out to do just that. He went to a king who was said to be very wealthy. Agastya told the king, 'I have come looking for wealth. Give me what you can spare.'

The king told the sage the exact income of his state and also the exact expenditure. Agastya was surprised to find that there was very little balance left. 'I can't possibly take that away. It belongs to the people,' said Agastya firmly. 'So I shall look elsewhere.'

The story goes that the king also accompanied Agastya on his mission. They visited two more kingdoms and in both places, they found the same state of affairs. Agastya was surprised to find that the powerful kshatriya kings were unwise enough to spend all the revenues of the state and not bother to save anything. He also realized that it was no use seeking alms from kings. So he decided to go to the rich but wicked Ilvala and try his luck there.

Ilvala and his brother Vatapi were fearsome demons who had a special dislike for humans. They loved to trap and kill humans and their method of doing so was quite novel. Ilvala would climb a tree and wait for someone to pass underneath. As soon as Ilvala saw a person approach, he jumped off the tree, took on the shape of a humble householder and threw himself at the man's feet. 'Maharaj,' he would beg, 'please honour my home by stepping into it. And please, please be gracious as to have a meal with me. Where else can I find a man as noble as you?'

Many men fell for this kind of flattery and happily followed Ilvala home to his cave. Once inside the cave, Ilvala chanted a spell that converted Vatapi into a goat. Those days meat-eating was quite common. So while the guest was waiting, Ilvala slaughtered the 'goat' and turned the meat into a fabulous meal. The poor, unsuspecting guest ate his fill, wondering at this stroke of luck. As soon as he had finished, Ilvala chanted another spell that brought Vatapi back to life. Out came Vatapi, tearing his way through the victim's stomach. He was all in one piece but the guest fell down dead. In this way, many innocent men had lost their lives.

When Ilvala learnt that Agastya had come to that part of the country and was making enquiries about him, he was delighted. Agastya was a distinguished sage and here he was, all ready to walk into the trap! What could be better? So Ilvala hurried to welcome Agastya. Knowing the sage's powers, he did not take on human form but remained a demon. 'Rishivar,' said Ilvala, 'How fortunate I am to have you in my neighbourhood today! Please be so kind as to have a meal with me. My home shall be purified by your very presence!'

Agastya followed Ilvala to the cave. As usual, Ilvala turned Vatapi into a goat, killed the goat and laid on a splendid feast. When Agastya had eaten his fill, Ilvala repeated the magic spell and shouted aloud, 'Vatapi, come out!' But Agastya smiled, rubbed his stomach gently and said, 'O Vatapi, be digested in my stomach for the peace and good of the world!'

Ilvala was getting anxious about the safety of his brother. He shouted again, 'Vatapi, come out!' But nothing happened. Frantic by now, Ilvala shouted a third time, with no result. And Agastya explained why. Vatapi had simply been digested! Ilvala's evil plan was finally defeated. He bowed to Agastya and surrendered to him all the wealth that the sage required. Agastya came back to Lopamudra and was at last able to provide her with the comforts that she desired.

The legend goes on to say that at one time the Vindhyachal mountains became jealous of Mount Meru, the abode of the gods, which is in heaven. The Vindhyas began to grow in height so they could be taller than Mount Meru and blot out the sun, moon and stars. The gods realized the danger and begged of Agastya to help.

The sage went to the Vindhyas and said, 'O greatest of mountains, please stop growing for a while. I am on my way to the south and must cross you. When I have returned north again, you are free to grow as much as you like. But till then, be so kind as to wait.'

Agastya was so highly respected that the Vindhyas listened to him. He crossed them on his way to the south, but never returned north again. Instead, he settled down in the south. The Vindhyas waited for him indefinitely. And that is exactly why they did not grow any taller!

Bhim and Hanuman

The two famous epics, the Ramayan and the Mahabharat are distinct and separate. It is believed that the events of the Mahabharat took place some five hundred to one thousand years after those of the Ramayan. The locations and the characters of the two epics are different too. But here is a unique story which combines characters from both these epics, Hanuman from the Ramayan and Bhim from the Mahabharat.

Hanuman is the monkey god so widely worshipped in India. He is believed to be a great devotee of Lord Ram. He had strength enough to carry a mountain on his shoulders. Capable of growing at will, he could become taller than any giant and is believed to have crossed the ocean in one leap.

Bhim was the second of the five Pandava brothers of Mahabharat fame. He was also known for his giant physique and enormous strength.

*

The Pandavas were exiled to the forest for a period of twelve years by their enemies, the Kauravas. During these twelve years the Pandavas moved from one forest to another. Wherever they found fresh water and a suitable place to build an ashram, they stopped for some time. Once they came to the forest of Narayanashram and halted there. It was indeed a charming place, with shady green trees surrounding a wide open space. The holy river Ganga flowed nearby and was a great source of joy to them all. A bath in the sparkling cold water of the Ganga cleared the mind and removed all traces of fatigue.

Draupadi, in particular, was very happy living on the bank of the Ganga. After a bath early in the morning, she would stand in the water and worship the sun god with offerings of fresh fruit and flowers. One day, as Draupadi finished her prayers and waded into the river, a breeze sprang up from the north-east. And floating on the breeze came a flower that dropped near Draupadi. It was a beautiful flower, with a hundred velvety petals, golden in colour. And the fragrance was heavenly.

Draupadi uttered a cry of joy. She picked up the flower and ran to Bhim. 'I'm sure you've never seen anything so beautiful,' she said. 'What a colour! What a lovely scent! Oh Bhim, get me more flowers like this. Promise me you will.'

Bhim promised, though he had no idea where he would find such flowers. Draupadi was so dear to him that he was quite willing to go to the four corners of the earth for something to please her. He immediately set out in the direction from which the breeze was blowing, without stopping to think of the dangers that lay ahead.

For a long time Bhim walked along the river till he came to the foot of a mountain. Spread out before him was a grove of plantain trees. A path ran through the grove. And lying across the path, blocking it completely, was a monkey. But it was no ordinary monkey. Huge in size, he shone like a blazing fire. Bhim was a little surprised to see the monkey. He tried to frighten the animal out of the way by shouting at him. But the monkey did not move at all. He only opened his eyes a little and said in a sleepy voice, 'I'm lying here because I'm not feeling well. Why did you wake me up? You are a human being. Shouldn't human beings be more kind and considerate towards animals? Who are you and where are you going?'

Bhim was not used to people talking to him in this manner. He grew very angry and shouted, 'What right have you to ask all these questions? You are only a monkey while I am a kshatriya

born of the illustrious Kuru dynasty. Do you know, you ignorant monkey, that I am a son of the great and powerful wind god himself? Now move out of my way and let me go.'

The monkey heard him but made no attempt to move. He simply smiled and said, 'I may be only a monkey as you say. But heed my warning. Don't try to force your way past me or you shall meet your doom.'

At this Bhim grew even more angry. 'How does it matter to you if I meet my doom? And move out of my way or I shall force you to do so.'

'Why must you trouble me?' replied the monkey. 'I'm too old to move. Why don't you jump over me instead?'

Bhim replied, 'That is something I will not do because the scriptures forbid it. Otherwise I could easily jump over you like Hanuman leaping over the sea to reach Lanka.'

The monkey looked greatly surprised. 'Hanuman?' he repeated. 'Who is this Hanuman that you speak of? Do tell me.'

Bhim replied with great pride. 'Hanuman is also a son of the great wind god. He is my elder brother. Once he crossed the ocean in a single giant leap. Have you ever heard of a thing like that? But remember, I am equal to him in strength. So if you don't get up and make way for me, you will be sorry. . . .'

The monkey replied, 'You may be very strong but you must also learn to be patient with the old and the weak. I don't have the strength to move and you don't wish to jump over me. So why not move aside my tail and make way for yourself?'

Here was some action and Bhim loved action. He was so proud of his strength that he laughed at the thought of moving the monkey's tail to make a path for himself. It would be child's play. But there was a great shock in store for Bhim. He could not move the monkey's tail by so much as the breadth of a single hair. He tried his hardest, using all his strength, but nothing happened. He set his jaws and strained every muscle till the very sinews seemed to crack and perspiration ran down his body. But he could not move the tail one little bit, up or down or sideways. For the first time in his life, Bhim felt humbled. He folded his hands and begged forgiveness. 'Forgive me my arrogance in thinking I was superior to you in strength. O great one, tell me who you are—rishi or a god or some other divine being?'

The monkey replied, 'O Bhim, I am none other than your brother Hanuman. Like you, I am a son of the powerful wind god. Welcome, my brother. How wonderful it is to meet you and to see how strong you are!'

As for Bhim, he was delighted beyond words. Throwing himself at the feet of Hanuman he cried, 'How fortunate I am to have met you at last! All my life I have longed to set eyes on my brother Hanuman who is worshipped as a devotee of Ram and as a god who relieves the suffering of mankind. My brother, I long to see the form in which you leapt across the ocean. Please let me have the honour.'

At this Hanuman smiled and began to increase in size. Very soon he stood as tall as a mountain, seeming to fill the entire landscape. Bhim was completely overawed by the sight. He covered his eyes with both hands because the light that radiated from the figure of Hanuman was simply dazzling.

'Bhim,' said Hanuman, 'in the presence of my enemies my body can grow larger still.'

But soon Hanuman got back to his normal size again. He embraced Bhim. There was so much divine power in him that his very embrace filled Bhim with strength. He felt refreshed and completely recovered from the effect of his long, tiring walk.

Hanuman said, 'I lay here blocking your path for a very special reason. Beyond this grove of plantain trees lies the world of spirits and yakshas (semi-divine beings). They don't welcome human beings. If you enter their world, you shall run into great danger. So go back the way you came.'

'What about the flowers I came looking for?' returned Bhim. 'Draupadi wants me to get her some flowers.'

'I know,' said Hanuman. 'The name of that flower is saugandhika, and it grows in a stream close by. You can pick as many as you like. But before we part, I wish to bless you.'

Bhim stood before his elder brother, head bowed, eyes closed and hands folded in respect. Hanuman said, 'You will soon be fighting your enemies, the Kauravas, to regain your kingdom. I shall not be there in person but I shall lend you my strength. When you challenge the enemy on the field of battle, my voice shall join yours and strike terror into their hearts! Victory shall be yours!'

Bhim touched Hanuman's feet and thanked him. Then he went towards the stream where the saugandhika flowers grew. He gathered an armful of flowers and hurried back home. Draupadi was waiting. She was delighted to get the flowers and thanked Bhim for all the trouble he had taken to get them for her.

Bhasmasura

It is believed that long, long ago, there were a lot of asuras or demons living on earth. These asuras were both wicked and dangerous. They killed innocent people just for the fun of it. Everyone was afraid of them. Even the lesser gods were afraid and looked up to the more powerful gods—Brahma, Vishnu and Mahesh (Shiva)—for protection. Many of our old legends tell us how a particular asura was overpowered and killed by the gods.

The story of Bhasmasura comes to us from ancient books called the Puranas, which are a storehouse of old, traditional tales. These tales used to be told orally, by old people and professional story-tellers. But around the 8th century A.D. they were put down in writing.

*

Bhasmasura was a demon, a cunning and wicked demon. He had only one aim in life—to become the most powerful person on earth. He wished everyone else to be afraid of him and to acknowledge him king.

But how could his wish come true? He had neither the courage nor the strength to fight and conquer and become a king. For a long time Bhasmasura thought over it. At last he hit upon a plan. He decided to become a devotee of Lord Shiva. Once Lord Shiva was pleased with him, it would be simple to ask for a boon. And by way of a boon Bhasmasura would ask for magical powers. He would ask for something that would straightaway make him the most powerful person on earth.

Having made this plan, Bhasmasura went away to a dense forest. He sat down under a tree and began to pray to Lord Shiva.

Bhasmasura prayed for a long, long time. Some say that he prayed for years on end. At length Lord Shiva appeared before him and said, 'I am pleased with your devotion. Ask for any boon and it shall be granted.'

The crafty Bhasmasura fell at the feet of the all-powerful Shiva. 'O lord,' he said, 'I only seek your blessings. If I have your blessings, what else is left to ask for?'

'Even so,' replied Lord Shiva, 'you have only to name the boon and it shall be granted.'

For a moment Bhasmasura seemed lost in thought. Then he said in all humility, 'Grant me the power to destroy my enemies. Let it come to pass that when I place my right hand on the head of another, he should be reduced to ashes.'

'That is a strange request. But you already have my word for it. The boon is granted!'

Bhasmasura's head suddenly jerked up. There was a wicked gleam in his eyes. 'My lord,' he said, 'permit me to test the strength of the boon on the giver of the boon!' And, right hand outstretched, he leapt after Lord Shiva. But he stumbled over a stone and fell. When he looked up again, Lord Shiva was gone.

Bhasmasura now started his reign of terror on earth. He always walked with his right hand outstretched and destroyed people right and left. Enemies, friends, kings and commoners—they were all reduced to ashes. And each time this happened Bhasmasura laughed his hoarse and wicked laugh and shouted, 'I am Bhasmasura, the great demon. There's nobody on earth more powerful than I.'

Not content with destroying people, Bhasmasura turned his attention to the gods in heaven. Climbing snowclad peaks and leaping over rivers was child's play for him. Soon he was in heaven and the lesser gods ran to Lord Shiva who lived on Mount Kailash. 'O lord,' they begged, 'please take the boon back. Bhasmasura is out to destroy us.' But so great was the power of the boon granted by Lord Shiva that he himself could not take it back. He could have destroyed Bhasmasura, but did not wish to do so since the demon had once been his devotee.

The lesser gods ran to Vishnu. 'O lord,' said the gods in one voice, 'save us from Bhasmasura. He has received a boon from Lord Shiva. He can reduce a person to ashes simply by placing his right hand on the other's head. If you don't help us, we shall all be finished.'

'Hm,' said Vishnu. 'Bhasmasura has been given this boon by Shiva, you say? If it is granted by Shiva then I myself cannot take it away.'

'Please, please help us,' the gods begged again. Unable to turn down their request, Vishnu thought for a long while and said, 'All right, all right. You can go back and leave this to me.' One last bow and the gods went away.

Meanwhile Bhasmasura was charging up the main road of heaven. He looked right and left, trying to find someone whom he could reduce to ashes. But heaven was empty. The palaces and gardens stood silent, without a trace of life. All the gods and goddesses had gone into hiding. 'Where is everyone?' roared Bhasmasura. 'Come out and bow to the greatest of the great, the unconquerable Bhasmasura.'

A voice, sweet as the tinkling of a silver bell, interrupted him. 'What is all this noise about?'

Bhasmasura turned in the direction of the sound and stood rooted to the spot. There, right in front of him, stood the most beautiful young woman that he had ever seen. She was tall and slender and her face seemed to glow through the veil that fell over her forehead. Bhasmasura stared at her for a long time. At last he managed to find his voice. 'Who. . . who are you?' he asked.

'My name is Mohini,' she replied. 'I live with my parents in the forest nearby. But you look all tired and dusty. You must have been travelling for a long time. Won't you come and rest for a while? My house is not to far from here.'

She talked and he listened. And as she moved away, he followed as in a dream. Mohini seemed to float over the ground. After a while they came to an open meadow and Mohini sat down to rest on a rock. Bhasmasura was waiting for just such an opportunity. He went down on his knees before her, folded his hands and begged, 'I love you, Mohini. Will you marry me?'

Mohini laughed outright. Her laugh was even sweeter than her smile. At the very sound of it, Bhasmasura fell even more deeply in love with her. 'Why do you laugh?' he asked.

'I'm not so foolish as to marry you,' she retorted. 'Who knows how many wives you already have, tucked away back home?'

'Not a single one, I promise you,' cried Bhasmasura, quick to defend himself. 'I'm still a most eligible bachelor!'

Mohini looked him up and down. Then she turned up her nose again saying, 'Hm. It is possible that I shall be your first wife. But what is to prevent you from marrying a hundred more later on?'

Quite desperate by now, Bhasmasura declared, 'If you marry me, I promise I won't ever take a second wife.'

'How can I trust you?'

'But you must. I love you, Mohini. How can I marry another?'

'Very well, then you must take an oath on that.'

'I swear that if you marry me, I won't take a second wife,' said Bhasmasura, only too eager to please.

'That is no way to take an oath,' said Mohini. 'Do it properly.'

'How do you mean?' asked Bhasmasura.

'Do exactly as I say,' said Mohini. 'First, face the rising sun.'

Bhasmasura faced the rising sun.

'Stand straight.'

Bhasmasura stood straight.

'Close your eyes.'

Bhasmasura closed his eyes.

'Now place your right hand on your head and say, "I swear on my honour I shall never take a second wife."'

Bhasmasura placed his right hand on his head and lo, before he could utter a single word, he was reduced to a heap of ashes!

That very minute Mohini also changed her shape. In place of a beautiful young woman stood a smiling Lord Vishnu. And from all four corners of heaven, the lesser gods began to pour in to thank him for saving their lives.